NINJA
DUAL ZONE
AIR FRYER
COOKBOOK

1200 | DAYS EASY AND DELICIOUS AIR FRYER RECIPES TO GRILL BAKE, ROAST AND FRY MEALS IN 2-BASKET AT SAME TIME

Edwin Roman

Legal & Disclaimer

The content and information in this book is consistent and truthful, and it has been provided for informational, educational and business purposes only.

The illustrations in the book are from the website shutterstock.com, depositphoto.com and freepik.com and have been authorized.

The content and information contained in this book has been compiled from reliable sources, which are accurate based on the knowledge, belief, expertise and information of the Author. The author cannot be held liable for any omissions and/or errors.

Table of Content

INTRODUCTION

If you are looking for a magical kitchen appliance to cook like a ninja, the Ninja Dual Zone Air Fryer is an excellent tool for you to serve you. You can prepare all types of your favorite dishes in minutes and can make the ready within a few seconds. The dual zone technology allows you to cook different foods simultaneously in two different baskets. Its saves time and cook foods quickly which require more time to be prepared separately. It Is a great appliance to making

almost every kind of food including French fries, nuggets, pork chops, baked items, beef steaks, fish fillets, roasted vegetables, and other tongue satisfying food items without worried of food to get greasy and or soaked into a lot of oil. You can use it as an air fryer to cook food without or with very little usage of oil and can have highly crispy and golden food items, while, the other feature of the Ninja Dual Zone Air Fryer helps you to cook food as an oven cooked food for baking different kinds of foods. It is a best cooking appliance for all those who want to cook food and love to share it with others. It helps to make highly healthy food as well as most delicious recipes.

In this cookbook, you will learn the background of the Ninja Dual Zone Air Fryer, benefits of using the air fryer for cooking healthy meals, setting up the Ninja Dual Zone Air Fryer, tips for using the air fryer effectively, proper cleaning and maintenance of the air fryer, and delicious recipes.

The Ninja Dual Zone Air Fryer is a versatile appliance that offers a range of features to help you cook delicious and healthy meals. Here are some of its key features:

1.Dual Zone Technology: The Ninja Dual Zone Air Fryer allows you to cook two different dishes at the same time, each with their own temperature and cooking time. This is perfect for preparing a main dish and a side dish at the same time, or for cooking multiple items for a larger group.

2.Large Capacity: With a 8-quart capacity, the Ninja Dual Zone Air Fryer is larger than many traditional air fryers, which allows you to cook bigger batches of food or multiple dishes at once.

3.Digital Display: The air fryer has a digital display that makes it easy to set the temperature and cooking time, and to monitor the progress of your food.

4.Multiple Cooking Functions: The Ninja Dual Zone Air Fryer has a range of cooking functions, including air fry, roast, reheat, dehydrate, bake, and broil. This versatility allows you to cook a wide variety of dishes using just one appliance.

5.Customizable Cooking Settings: You can customize the cooking settings on the air fryer to suit your needs, including adjusting the temperature and cooking time for each zone, and choosing between different cooking methods.

6.Easy to Clean: The air fryer has non-stick surfaces and dishwasher-safe parts, making it easy to clean up after use.

7.Safety Features: The air fryer has safety features, such as an automatic shut-off function, to prevent overcooking and ensure that the appliance is safe to use.

The Ninja Dual Zone Air Fryer Cookbook is a comprehensive guide that features a collection of recipes specially curated for use with the Ninja Dual Zone Air Fryer. This cookbook covers a wide range of recipes for different mealtimes of the day, including breakfast, lunch, dinner, snacks, and desserts, which have been carefully crafted and tested by professional chefs.

The cookbook has been designed to help users maximize the benefits of their air fryer while exploring diverse culinary options. Each recipe includes detailed step-by-step instructions on how to prepare and cook the dish, as well as information on the recommended cooking temperature and time. Some recipes also come with helpful tips and tricks to achieve the best possible results.

Furthermore, the cookbook includes useful information on how to use and maintain the Ninja Dual Zone Air Fryer, which can be particularly beneficial for beginners or those looking to improve their cooking skills. The Ninja Dual Zone Air Fryer Cookbook is an excellent resource for anyone who owns a Ninja Dual Zone Air Fryer and wants to broaden their culinary horizons. With its broad range of recipes and helpful tips, this cookbook can assist users in creating delectable, nutritious meals with ease. I hope you find this book a great guide in your journey of using your Ninja Dual Zone Air Fryer.

All about Background of Ninja Dual Zone Air Fryer

The Ninja Dual Zone Air Fryer serves a unique feature of having two separate 4L baskets that operate independently, allowing you to prepare two different dishes simultaneously, unlike conventional single-basket air fryers that require sequential cooking. Additionally, it offers six versatile programs, including Air Broil, Air Fry, Roast, Bake, Reheat, and Dehydrate. The appliance has a smart function that synchronizes the cooking duration in each zone, enabling distinct meals to be ready simultaneously. The Ninja Dual air fryer left me thoroughly impressed with its sturdiness and versatility. Its attractive design features two capacious drawers and detachable non-stick crisper plates, while its matte grey exterior is accentuated with sleek stainless-steel components of superior quality. Notably, the appliance is effortless to operate as an air fryer, and its multiple functionalities encompass roasting, baking, reheating, dehydrating fruits and vegetables, and using the air fry function to transform frozen food into crispy delights within minutes. Furthermore, the manufacturer claims a 75% reduction in energy consumption compared to traditional air frying methods.

Nearly eighty years ago, William Maxson invented and developed the original concept of the air fryer to reheat frozen meals for American service members while they were deployed. This concept evolved over time and eventually became the air fryer that we know today. The history of the air fryer is rooted in scientific discoveries, which were primarily driven by two men who were unhappy with the quality of their frozen food. Today, the air fryer is widely used for cooking, heating, and frying foods, without the need for fatty oils and greases typically used in traditional frying methods. As a result, it has become one of the most popular appliances in America today. In the early twentieth century, owning a freezer was a luxury that very few people could afford. William Maxson, an army veteran, was an early adopter of freezing food, even before refrigerators were commonplace. However, the thawing process or baking the food in an oven took a considerable amount of time and made it inconvenient for his fellow soldiers during World War II, who had to eat cold sandwiches or non-perishable food while on missions.

Maxson developed a "whirlwind oven" that used a fan to blow hot air onto the food, evenly heating it without burning or leaving the center cold. He patented the invention and sold it to the US Army, allowing pilots and service people to have hot meals while flying. This early version of the air fryer became popular until the invention of the microwave, which offered a quicker way of heating food.

Fast forward to the early 2000s, Fred van der Weij was unhappy with how fried food tasted when heated in a microwave or oven. Deep fryers were both expensive and unhealthy, so van der Weij used Maxson's fan and hot air technology to create what we now know as the air fryer. He partnered with Philips to release a personal air fryer in 2010, which quickly became a success.

The air fryer's popularity lies in its ease of use and compatibility with modern life, as it can cook food in under half an hour with less time, energy, and dishes than regular oven or stovetop cooking. Today, around 40% of American households own an air fryer, as they seek healthier options for fried foods and cook from home more. The air fryer's popularity soared during the Covid-19 pandemic. Therefore, the air fryer we use today is a combination of the efforts of two men: William Maxson and Fred van der Weij, who saw an opportunity to create a better way to heat and cook food.

Benefits of Using the Ninja Dual Zone Air Fryer

The Ninja Dual Zone Air Fryer has some distinct advantages over a traditional air fryer. Here are some of the benefits of using the Ninja Dual Zone Air Fryer:

1.Dual Zone Technology: One of the biggest advantages of the Ninja Dual Zone Air Fryer is its dual zone technology, which allows you to cook two separate dishes at different temperatures and times simultaneously. This feature can save you time and energy when preparing meals, especially when cooking for a family or group of people.

2.Larger Capacity: The Ninja Dual Zone Air Fryer has a larger capacity than many traditional air fryers, allowing you to cook larger portions of food or multiple dishes at once. This can be particularly useful for preparing meals for a larger group of people or for batch cooking.

3.Versatility: The Ninja Dual Zone Air Fryer is a versatile appliance that can be used for a variety of cooking methods, including air frying, baking, roasting, and dehydrating. This versatility can save you money and space in the kitchen by eliminating the need for multiple appliances.

4.Customizable Cooking Settings: The Ninja Dual Zone Air Fryer allows you to customize your cooking settings to achieve the perfect texture and flavor for your food. You can adjust the temperature, time, and cooking method to suit your preferences and dietary needs.

5.Easy to Clean: The Ninja Dual Zone Air Fryer is designed for easy cleaning, with non-stick surfaces and removable parts that can be washed in the dishwasher. This makes it a convenient and low-maintenance appliance to have in your kitchen.

Overall, the Ninja Dual Zone Air Fryer offers many advantages over a traditional air fryer, including dual zone technology, larger capacity, versatility, customizable cooking settings, and easy cleaning.

Getting Started the Ninja Dual Zone Air Fryer

Getting started with cooking in the Ninja Dual Zone Air Fryer is easy! Here are some basic steps to follow:

1.Read the manual: Before you start cooking, it's important to read the user manual and familiarize yourself with the controls and functions of the appliance.

2.Preheat the air fryer: Depending on the recipe, preheat the air fryer to the appropriate temperature for the food you will be cooking. Preheating helps ensure that your food cooks evenly and to the right temperature.

3.Prepare the food: Prep your ingredients as directed in the recipe. Some recipes may require you to add oil or seasoning to your food before cooking.

4.Place the food in the air fryer: Once the air fryer is preheated, place your food in the cooking basket. Be sure not to overcrowd the basket as this can affect the cooking process.

5.Set the cooking time and temperature: Using the digital controls, set the cooking time and temperature according to the recipe. The cooking time may vary depending on the type and quantity of food being cooked.

6.Monitor the cooking process: Keep an eye on the food as it cooks, and adjust the temperature or cooking time if necessary. If you're cooking two different foods at once, be sure to check on both zones periodically.

7.Remove and serve the food: Once the food is cooked to your liking, use tongs or a spatula to carefully remove it from the air fryer. Allow it to cool for a few minutes before serving.

With these basic steps, you can start cooking a wide variety of delicious and healthy meals in your Ninja Dual Zone Air Fryer. Be sure to experiment with different types of food and seasonings to find your favorite recipes.

You can cook a wide range of foods in the Ninja Dual Zone Air Fryer. Some examples include:

1.Chicken wings   2.French fries

3.Fried chicken   4.Fish fillets

5.Roasted vegetables   6.Pork chops

7.Shrimp   8.Hamburgers

9.Baked potatoes   10.Onion rings

11.Mozzarella sticks   12.Doughnuts

13.Apple chips   14.Beef jerky

15.Kale chips

These are just a few examples, but the Ninja Dual Zone Air Fryer is a versatile appliance that can be used to cook many different types of foods.

The detail of using the Ninja air fryer cooker in both zones for cooking the delicious meals is given in the below section.

Setting up the Ninja Dual Zone Air Fryer

You can use the Ninja Dual Zone Air Fryer to cook two different foods at the same time, even if they don't need to finish cooking at the same time. Here's how:

1.Place the food you want to cook in either the cooking pot or basket, depending on the size and type of food you are cooking.

2.Place the cooking basket into one of the cooking zones (the default is Zone 1).

3.Select the cooking function you want to use, such as Air Fry, by pressing the corresponding button on the control panel.

4.Set the temperature and cooking time using the digital controls on the front of the air fryer. You can adjust the settings for either Zone 1 or Zone 2 by pressing the "Zone" button to select the desired zone.

5.Press the start button to begin cooking.

During cooking, you can open the top cover of the air fryer to check on the food and shake the basket if necessary, to ensure even cooking. If you are cooking two different foods in the two different zones, you can set different cooking times and temperatures for each zone to ensure they cook properly. Once the cooking time has elapsed, the air fryer will automatically turn off. Open the top cover and use the handles on the basket to remove the food from the air fryer.

If you're only cooking one thing, you can fill a single zone in the Ninja Dual Zone Air Fryer and use it like a traditional air fryer by filling up your cooking basket with desired food and selecting the time and temperature from the touch panel. Let the food cook and shake the basket in different intervals while food is cooking. Using a single zone in the Ninja Dual Zone Air Fryer is a great option if you only need to cook one thing, as it allows you to use the air fryer like a traditional air fryer, but with the added benefit of being able to cook two different foods simultaneously if needed you can use the other option.

Tips for Using the Air Fryer Effectively

Here are some effective tips to use your Ninja Dual Zone Air Fryer:

* Preheat the air fryer: Before cooking, preheat the air fryer for a few minutes to ensure even cooking and a crispy texture. Most air fryers have a preheat function that you can use.

* Avoid overcrowding: Overcrowding the cooking basket can hinder proper air circulation, resulting in unevenly cooked food. Leave some space between each piece to ensure even cooking.

* Use oil sparingly: Air frying requires less oil than traditional frying but adding too much oil can make your food greasy and unhealthy. Lightly coat your food with oil using a spray bottle or oil mister for better control.

* Shake the basket: Periodically shake the basket to ensure all sides of the food are exposed to the hot air and to ensure even cooking.

* Experiment with cooking times and temperatures: Every air fryer is different, so you may need to experiment with cooking times and temperatures to find what works best for you. Start with the recommended settings but be willing to adjust as needed based on your experience.

* Clean regularly: Regularly clean your air fryer to ensure it works properly and to prevent unwanted flavors from being absorbed into your food. Most air fryers have dishwasher-safe parts but be sure to follow the manufacturer's instructions. By following these tips, you can maximize the performance of your Ninja Dual Zone Air Fryer and enjoy delicious, healthy meals with ease.

Proper Cleaning and Maintenance of the Air Fryer

To ensure that your Ninja Dual Zone air fryer works properly and keeps up its performance, it is essential to clean and maintain it regularly. Below are some guidelines to help you keep your air fryer in good condition:

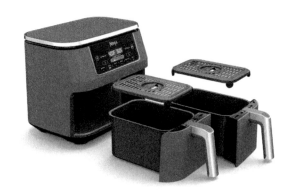

1.Allow the air fryer to cool completely before cleaning and unplug it from the power source.

2.Remove all removable parts, such as cooking baskets and crisper plates, from the air fryer.

3.Wash the removable parts with warm, soapy water or put them in the dishwasher if they are dishwasher safe.

4.Wipe the interior and exterior of the air fryer with a damp cloth. Avoid using abrasive sponges or cleaners that can damage the surface.

5.For tough stains or stubborn food particles, use a non-abrasive cleaner that is specially designed for air fryers.

6.Dry all the parts thoroughly before reassembling the air fryer.

7.Regularly check the heating element and fan for any buildup of grease or debris. Use a soft-bristled brush or a damp cloth to clean these areas carefully.

8.Store the air fryer in a cool and dry place when not in use.

By following these steps, you can maintain your Ninja Dual Zone air fryer's performance, extend its lifespan, and ensure that your food always tastes great. It is crucial to follow the manufacturer's instructions and guidelines for cleaning and maintenance.

Conclusion

The Ninja Dual Zone Air Fryer is a highly versatile appliance that can efficiently cook a variety of foods. Its dual-zone technology allows for the simultaneous cooking of two different foods at different temperatures and times, making it perfect for busy households or multitasking chefs. The air fryer function uses hot air to cook food to a crispy, golden brown texture with little to no oil or fat. This appliance can also be used for baking, roasting, and dehydrating, providing a range of cooking options in one device.

The Ninja Dual Zone Air Fryer is a great choice for those seeking a versatile kitchen tool that can replace multiple appliances. It can cook anything from chicken wings to vegetables to homemade chips, and its digital controls make selecting the appropriate cooking function and temperature a breeze. Moreover, the removable parts make cleaning and maintenance hassle-free.

Overall, if you're looking to save time and effort in the kitchen while still producing healthy and delicious meals, the Ninja Dual Zone Air Fryer is definitely a valuable investment to consider.

BASIC KITCHEN CONVERSIONS & EQUIVALENTS

DRY MEASUREMENTS CONVERSION CHART

3 teaspoons = 1 tablespoon = 1/16 cup

6 teaspoons = 2 tablespoons = 1/8 cup

12 teaspoons = 4 tablespoons = ¼ cup

24 teaspoons = 8 tablespoons = ½ cup

36 teaspoons = 12 tablespoons = ¾ cup

48 teaspoons = 16 tablespoons = 1 cup

METRIC TO US COOKING CONVERSIONS

OVEN TEMPERATURES

120 ºC = 250 ºF   160 ºC = 320 ºF

180 ºC = 350 ºF   205 ºC = 400 ºF

220 ºC = 425 ºF

LIQUID MEASUREMENTS CONVERSION CHART

8 fluid ounces = 1 cup = ½ pint = ¼ quart

16 fluid ounces = 2 cups = 1 pint = ½ quart

32 fluid ounces = 4 cups = 2 pints = 1 quart = ¼ gallon

128 fluid ounces = 16 cups = 8 pints = 4 quarts = 1 gallon

BAKING IN GRAMS

1 cup flour = 140 grams

1 cup sugar = 150 grams

1 cup powdered sugar = 160 grams

1 cup heavy cream = 235 grams

VOLUME

1 milliliter = 1/5 teaspoon

5 ml = 1 teaspoon   15 ml = 1 tablespoon

240 ml = 1 cup or 8 fluid ounces

1 liter = 34 fluid ounces

WEIGHT

1 gram = .035 ounces

100 grams = 3.5 ounces

500 grams = 1.1 pounds

1 kilogram = 35 ounces

US TO METRIC COOKING CONVERSIONS

1/5 tsp = 1 ml   1 tsp = 5 ml

1 tbsp = 15 ml   1 fluid ounces = 30 ml

1 cup = 237 ml   1 pint (2 cups) = 473 ml

1 quart (4 cups) = .95 liter

1 gallon (16 cups) = 3.8 liters

1 oz = 28 grams   1 pound = 454 grams

BUTTER

1 cup butter = 2 sticks = 8 ounces = 230 grams = 16 tablespoons

WHAT DOES 1 CUP EQUAL

1 cup = 8 fluid ounces   1 cup = 16 tablespoons

1 cup = 48 teaspoons   1 cup = ½ pint

1 cup = ¼ quart   1 cup = 1/16 gallon

1 cup = 240 ml

BAKING PAN CONVERSIONS

9-inch round cake pan = 12 cups

10-inch tube pan =16 cups

10-inch bundt pan = 12 cups

9-inch springform pan = 10 cups

9 x 5 inch loaf pan = 8 cups

9-inch square pan = 8 cups

BAKING PAN CONVERSIONS

1 cup all-purpose flour = 4.5 oz

1 cup rolled oats = 3 oz

1 large egg = 1.7 oz

1 cup butter = 8 oz

1 cup milk = 8 oz

1 cup heavy cream = 8.4 oz

1 cup granulated sugar = 7.1 oz

1 cup packed brown sugar = 7.75 oz

1 cup vegetable oil = 7.7 oz

1 cup unsifted powdered sugar = 4.4 oz

CHAPTER 1 BREAKFAST

Bacon Hot Dogs

Prep time: 5 minutes, Cook time: 12 minutes, Serves 4

3 Brazilian sausages, cut into 3 equal pieces
9 slices bacon
1 tbsp. Italian herbs
Salt and ground black pepper, to taste

1. Take each slice of bacon and wrap around each piece of sausage. Sprinkle with Italian herbs, salt and pepper.
2. Install a crisper plate in a basket. Place sausages in the basket, then insert basket in unit.
3. Select Zone 1, select AIR FRY, set temperature to 200℃, and set time to 12 minutes. Press the START/PAUSE button to begin cooking.
4. With 6 minutes remaining, press START/PAUSE to pause the unit. Remove the basket from unit and f ip the sausages over. Reinsert basket in unit and press START/PAUSE to resume cooking.
5. When cooking is complete, remove basket from unit. Transfer sausages to a plate. Serve warm.

Delish Mushroom Frittata

Prep time: 15 minutes, Cook time: 17 minutes, Serves 2

½ red onion, sliced thinly
250g button mushrooms, sliced thinly
3 eggs   Cooking spray, as required

3 tbsps. feta cheese, crumbled   1 tbsp. olive oil
Salt, to taste

1. Grease two 10 cm ramekins with cooking spray.
2. Heat olive oil on medium heat in a frying pan and add onion and mushrooms.
3. Sauté for about 5 minutes and dish out the mushroom mixture in a bowl.
4. Whisk together eggs and salt in a small bowl and transfer into the prepared ramekins.
5. Place the mushroom mixture over the eggs and top with feta cheese.
6. Install a crisper plate in both baskets. Place one ramekin in each basket.
7. Select Zone 1, select BAKE, set temperature to 180℃, and set time to 12 minutes. Select MATCH COOK to match Zone 2 settings to Zone 1. Select START/PAUSE to begin cooking.
8. When cooking is complete, transfer ramekins and serve warm.

Pita and Pepperoni Pizza

Prep time: 10 minutes, Cook time: 8 minutes, Serves 1

1 tsp. olive oil   1 tbsp. pizza sauce   1 pita bread
6 pepperoni slices   ¼ tsp. garlic powder   ¼ tsp. dried oregano
60g grated Mozzarella cheese

1. Spread the pizza sauce on top of the pita bread. Put the pepperoni slices over the sauce, followed by the Mozzarella cheese.
2. Season with garlic powder and oregano.
3. Install a crisper plate in a basket. Grease the air fryer basket with olive oil. Place pita pizza in the basket, then insert basket in unit.
4. Select Zone 1, select BAKAE, set temperature to 180℃, and set time to 8 minutes. Press the START/PAUSE button to begin cooking.
5. When cooking is complete, remove basket from unit. Serve warm.

Bacon Eggs on the Go

Prep time: 5 minutes, Cook time: 15 minutes, Serves 1

2 eggs   110 g bacon, cooked   Salt and ground black pepper, to taste

1. Put liners in a regular cupcake tin.
2. Crack an egg into each of the cups and add the bacon. Season with some pepper and salt.
3. Install a crisper plate in a basket. Place 2 cups in the basket, then insert basket in unit.
4. Select Zone 1, select AIR FRY, set temperature to 200℃, and set time to 15 minutes. Press the START/PAUSE button to begin cooking, until the eggs are set.
5. When cooking is complete, remove basket from unit. Serve warm.

Classic British Breakfast

Prep time: 5 minutes, Cook time: 20 minutes, Serves 2

140g potatoes, sliced and diced   2 eggs   1 tbsp. olive oil
1 tin of baked beans   1 sausage   Salt, to taste

1. Break the eggs onto a 18 x 12 cm baking dish and sprinkle with salt.
2. Lay the beans on the dish, next to the eggs.
3. In a bowl, coat the potatoes with the olive oil. Sprinkle with salt.
4. Install a crisper plate in both baskets. Place potato slices in the Zone 1 basket, then insert basket in unit. Place the dish in the Zone 2 basket, then insert basket in unit.
5. Select Zone 1, select AIR FRY, set temperature to 200℃, and set time to 20 minutes. Select Zone 2, select BAKE, set temperature to 200℃, and set time to 16 minutes. Select SMART FINISH. Press the START/PAUSE button to begin cooking.
6. When the Zone 1 and 2 times reach 5 minutes, press START/PAUSE to pause the unit. Remove the baskets from unit. Slice up the sausage and throw the slices on top of the beans and eggs. Reinsert baskets in unit and press START/PAUSE to resume cooking.
7. When cooking is complete, serve immediately.

Quick Blueberry Muffins

Prep time: 10 minutes, Cook time: 15 minutes, Makes 8 muffins

170g flour   100g sugar   2 tsps. baking powder
¼ tsp. salt   80ml canola oil   1 egg
120ml milk
110g blueberries, fresh or frozen and thawed

1. In a medium bowl, stir together flour, sugar, baking powder, and salt.
2. In a separate bowl, combine oil, egg, and milk and mix well.
3. Add egg mixture to dry ingredients and stir just until moistened.
4. Gently stir in the blueberries.
5. Spoon batter evenly into parchment-paper-lined muffin cups.
6. Install a crisper plate in both baskets. Place 4 muffin cups in each basket.
7. Select Zone 1, select BAKAE, set temperature to 180°C, and set time to 15 minutes. Select MATCH COOK to match Zone 2 settings to Zone 1. Select START/PAUSE to begin cooking, until tops spring back when touched lightly.
8. When cooking is complete, transfer muffin cups and serve warm.

Breakfast Creamy Doughnuts

Prep time: 10 minutes, Cook time: 16 minutes, Serves 8

cooking spray   1½ tsps. baking powder   1 pinch baking soda   120g sour cream
4 tbsps. butter, softened and divided   65g caster sugar   1 tsp. cinnamon 1
2 large egg yolks   280g plain flour   100g sugar   tsp. salt

1. Mix together sugar and butter in a bowl and beat until crumbly mixture is formed.
2. Whisk in the egg yolks and beat until well combined.
3. Sift together flour, baking powder, baking soda and salt in another bowl.
4. Add the flour mixture and sour cream to the sugar mixture.
5. Mix well to form a dough and refrigerate it.
6. Roll the dough into 5 cm thickness and cut the dough in half.
7. Coat both sides of the dough with the melted butter.
8. Install a crisper plate in both baskets. Spray with cooking spray. Place one dough in each basket.
9. Select Zone 1, select Bake, set temperature to 180°C, and set time to 16 minutes. Select MATCH COOK to match Zone 2 settings to Zone 1. Select START/PAUSE to begin cooking.
10. When cooking is complete, sprinkle the doughnuts with the cinnamon and caster sugar to serve.

Kale and Potato Nuggets

Prep time: 10 minutes, Cook time: 18 minutes, Serves 4

1 tsp. extra virgin olive oil

1 clove garlic, minced

4 cups kale, rinsed and chopped

28 g potatoes, boiled and mashed

30 ml milk   Cooking spray

Salt and ground black pepper, to taste

1. In a frying pan over medium heat, sauté the garlic in the olive oil, until it turns golden brown. Sauté with the kale for an additional 3 minutes and remove from the heat.
2. Mix the mashed potatoes, kale and garlic in a bowl. Pour in the milk and sprinkle with salt and pepper.
3. Shape the mixture into nuggets and spritz with cooking spray.
4. Install a crisper plate in a basket. Place nuggets in the basket, then insert basket in unit.
5. Select Zone 1, select AIR FRY, set temperature to 200℃, and set time to 15 minutes. Press the START/PAUSE button to begin cooking.
6. With 7 minutes remaining, press START/PAUSE to pause the unit. Remove the basket from unit and flip the nuggets over. Reinsert basket in unit and press START/PAUSE to resume cooking.
7. When cooking is complete, remove basket from unit. Transfer nuggets to a plate. Serve warm.

Fast Coffee Doughnuts

Prep time: 5 minutes, Cook time: 8 minutes, Serves 6

30 g sugar   ½ tsp. salt   120 g flour   1 tsp. baking powder

20 g coffee   1 tbsp. aquafaba   1 tbsp. sunflower oil

1. In a large bowl, combine the sugar, salt, flour, and baking powder.
2. Add the coffee, aquafaba, and sunflower oil and mix until a dough is formed. Leave the dough to rest in and the refrigerator.
3. Remove the dough from the fridge and divide up, kneading each section into a doughnut.
4. Install a crisper plate in both baskets. Place half of the doughnuts in a single layer in each basket.
5. Select Zone 1, select BAKE, set temperature to 200℃, and set time to 8 minutes. Select MATCH COOK to match Zone 2 settings to Zone 1. Select START/PAUSE to begin cooking.
6. When cooking is complete, transfer doughnuts to a plate. Serve warm.

Egg in a Bread Basket

Prep time: 10 minutes, Cook time: 12 minutes, Serves 2

2 bread slices   1 bacon slice, chopped

4 tomato slices

1 tbsp. Mozzarella cheese, shredded

2 eggs   ½ tbsp. olive oil

⅛ tsp. maple syrup   ⅛ tsp. balsamic vinegar

¼ tsp. fresh parsley, chopped

Salt and black pepper, to taste

2 tbsps. mayonnaise

1. Grease two 10 cm ramekins lightly.
2. Place 1 bread slice in each prepared ramekin and add bacon and tomato slices.
3. Top evenly with the Mozzarella cheese and crack 1 egg in each ramekin.
4. Drizzle with balsamic vinegar and maple syrup and season with parsley, salt and black pepper.
5. Install a crisper plate in both baskets. Place one ramekin in each basket.
6. Select Zone 1, select BAKE, set temperature to 160℃, and set time to 12 minutes. Select MATCH COOK to match Zone 2 settings to Zone 1. Select START/PAUSE to begin cooking.
7. When cooking is complete, top with mayonnaise and serve immediately.

Gold Avocado

Prep time: 5 minutes, Cook time: 8 minutes, Serves 4

2 large avocados, sliced   ¼ tsp. paprika

Salt and ground black pepper, to taste

60 g whole wheat flour   2 eggs, beaten

120 g bread crumbs

1. Sprinkle paprika, salt and pepper on the slices of avocado.
2. Lightly coat the avocados with flour. Dredge them in the eggs, before covering with bread crumbs.
3. Install a crisper plate in a basket. Place avocados in the basket, then insert basket in unit.
4. Select Zone 1, select AIR FRY, set temperature to 200℃, and set time to 8 minutes. Press the START/PAUSE button to begin cooking.
5. With 4 minutes remaining, press START/PAUSE to pause the unit. Remove the basket from unit and flip the avocados over. Reinsert basket in unit and press START/PAUSE to resume cooking.
6. When cooking is complete, remove basket from unit. Transfer avocados to a plate. Serve warm.

Cornflakes Toast Sticks

Prep time: 10 minutes, Cook time: 8 minutes, Serves 4

2 eggs   120 ml milk   6 slices sandwich bread, each slice cut into 4 strips
⅛ tsp. salt   ½ tsp. pure vanilla extract   Maple syrup, for dipping   Cooking spray
60 g crushed cornflakes

1. In a small bowl, beat together the eggs, milk, salt, and vanilla.
2. Put crushed cornflakes on a plate or in a shallow dish.
3. Dip bread strips in egg mixture, shake off excess, and roll in cornflake crumbs.
4. Spray both sides of bread strips with cooking spray.
5. Install a crisper plate in both baskets. Place half of the bread strips in a single layer in each basket.
6. Select Zone 1, select AIR FRY, set temperature to 200℃, and set time to 8 minutes. Select MATCH COOK to match Zone 2 settings to Zone 1. Select START/PAUSE to begin cooking.
7. When the Zone 1 and 2 times reach 4 minutes, press START/PAUSE to pause the unit. Remove the baskets from unit and flip the bread strips over. Reinsert baskets in unit and press START/PAUSE to resume cooking.
8. When cooking is complete, transfer bread strips to a plate. Serve warm with maple syrup.

Cherry Tomato Frittata

Prep time: 10 minutes, Cook time: 12 minutes, Serves 2

½ of Italian sausage   1 tsp. fresh parsley, chopped   1 tbsp. olive oil
4 cherry tomatoes, halved   3 eggs   Salt and black pepper, to taste
1 tbsp. Parmesan cheese, shredded

1. Preheat the Air fryer to 180℃.
2. Place the sausage and tomatoes in a 18 x 12 cm baking dish.
3. Install a crisper plate in a basket. Place baking dish in the basket, then insert basket in unit.
4. Select Zone 1, select BAKE, set temperature to 180℃, and set time to 12 minutes. Press the START/PAUSE button to begin cooking.
5. Whisk together eggs with Parmesan cheese, oil, parsley, salt and black pepper and beat until combined.
6. With 6 minutes remaining, press START/PAUSE to pause the unit. Remove the basket from unit. Drizzle the cheese mixture over sausage and tomatoes. Reinsert baskets in unit and press START/PAUSE to resume cooking.
7. When cooking is complete, remove basket from unit. Serve warm.

Nut and Seed Muffins

Prep time: 15 minutes, Cook time: 14 minutes, Makes 8 muffins

75 g whole-wheat flour.   24 g oat bran

2 tbsps. flaxseed meal   50 g brown sugar   ½ tsp. baking soda

½ tsp. baking powder   ¼ tsp. salt   ½ tsp. cinnamon

120 ml buttermilk   2 tbsps. melted butter   1 egg

½ tsp. pure vanilla extract   75 g grated carrots   Cooking spray

40 g chopped pecans   40 g chopped walnuts

1 tbsp. pumpkin seeds   1 tbsp. sunflower seeds

Special Equipment:

16 foil muffin cups, paper liners removed

1. In a large bowl, stir together the flour, bran, flaxseed meal, sugar, baking soda, baking powder, salt, and cinnamon.

2. In a medium bowl, beat together the buttermilk, butter, egg, and vanilla. Pour into flour mixture and stir just until dry ingredients moisten. Do not beat.

3. Gently stir in carrots, nuts, and seeds.

4. Double up the foil cups so you have 8 total and spritz with cooking spray.

5. Install a crisper plate in both baskets. Place 4 foil cups in a single layer in each basket.

6. Select Zone 1, select BAKE, set temperature to 180℃, and set time to 14 minutes. Select MATCH COOK to match Zone 2 settings to Zone 1. Select START/PAUSE to begin cooking, until a toothpick inserted in centre comes out clean.

7. When cooking is complete, serve warm.

Posh Orange Rolls

Prep time: 15 minutes, Cook time: 10 minutes, Makes 8 rolls

85 g low-fat cream cheese   ¼ cup desiccated, sweetened coconut

1 tbsp. low-fat sour cream or plain yoghurt   Butter-flavoured cooking spray

2 tsps. sugar   ¼ tsp. pure vanilla extract   For the Orange Glaze:

¼ tsp. orange extract   40 g chopped walnuts   65 g icing sugar   1 tbsp. orange juice

1 can (8 count) organic crescent roll dough   ¼ tsp. orange extract   Dash of salt

¼ cup dried cranberries

1. Cut 2 rectangle pieces of parchment paper slightly smaller than the bottom of the air fryer basket. Set aside.

2. In a small bowl, combine the cream cheese, sour cream or yoghurt, sugar, and vanilla and orange extracts. Stir until smooth.

3. Separate crescent roll dough into 8 triangles and divide cream cheese mixture among them. Starting at wide end, spread cheese mixture to within 2 cm of point.

4. Sprinkle nuts and cranberries evenly over cheese mixture.

5. Starting at wide end, roll up triangles, then sprinkle with coconut, pressing in lightly to make it stick. Spray tops of rolls with butter-flavoured cooking spray.

6. Install a crisper plate in both baskets. Put parchment paper and arrange 4 rolls in a single layer in each basket.

7. Select Zone 1, select BAKE, set temperature to 150℃, and set time to 10 minutes. Select MATCH COOK to match Zone 2 settings to Zone 1. Select START/PAUSE to begin cooking.

8. In a small bowl, stir together ingredients for glaze and drizzle over warm rolls. Serve warm.

CHAPTER 2 POULTRY

Chicken with Veggies

Prep time: 20 minutes, Cook time: 28 minutes, Serves 2

4 small artichoke hearts, quartered
4 fresh large button mushrooms, quartered
½ small onion, cut in large chunks
2 skinless, boneless chicken breasts
2 tbsps. fresh parsley, chopped

2 garlic cloves, minced   2 tbsps. chicken broth
2 tbsps. red wine vinegar   2 tbsps. olive oil
1 tbsp. Dijon mustard   ⅛ tsp. dried thyme
⅛ tsp. dried basil
Salt and black pepper, as required

1. Mix the garlic, broth, vinegar, olive oil, mustard, thyme, and basil in a bowl.
2. Mix the artichokes, mushrooms, onions, salt, and black pepper in another bowl.
3. Install a crisper plate in both baskets. Place chicken breasts in the Zone 1 basket and spread half of the mustard mixture evenly on it, then insert basket in unit. Place vegetables in the Zone 2 basket, then insert basket in unit.
4. Select Zone 1, select AIR FRY, set temperature to 200°C, and set time to 28 minutes. Select Zone 2, select AIR FRY, set temperature to 200°C, and set time to 18 minutes. Select SMART FINISH. Press the START/PAUSE button to begin cooking.
5. When the Zone 1 and Zone 2 times reach 10 minutes, press START/PAUSE and remove baskets from unit. In Zone 1, coat the chicken breasts with the remaining mustard mixture and flip the side. In Zone 2, shake for 10 seconds. Reinsert baskets in unit and press START/PAUSE to resume cooking.
6. When cooking is complete, transfer chicken and vegetables to a plate. Serve garnished with parsley.

Easy Asian Turkey Meatballs

Prep time: 10 minutes, Cook time: 13-14 minutes, Serves 4

2 tbsps. peanut oil, divided   1 small onion, minced
40 g water chestnuts, finely chopped   1 egg, beaten
½ tsp. ground ginger   40 g panko bread crumbs
2 tbsps. low-sodium soy sauce   450 g turkey mince

1. In a frying pan, heat 1 tbsp. of peanut oil until hot. Add onion and cook for 1 to 2 minutes o until crisp and tender. Transfer the onion to a medium bowl.
2. Place the water chestnuts, ground ginger, soy sauce, and bread crumbs to the onion and mix well. Add egg and stir well. Mix in the turkey mince until combined.
3. Form the mixture into 2 cm meatballs. Drizzle the remaining 1 tbsp. of oil over the meatballs.
4. Install a crisper plate in both baskets. Place half of meatballs in a single layer in each basket.
5. Select Zone 1, select BAKE, set temperature to 190°C, and set time to 12 minutes. Select MATCH COOK to match Zone 2 settings to Zone 1. Select START/PAUSE to begin cooking.
6. When the Zone 1 and 2 times reach 6 minutes, press START/PAUSE to pause the unit. Remove the baskets from unit and flip the meatballs over. Reinsert baskets in unit and press START/PAUSE to resume cooking.
7. When cooking is complete, transfer meatballs to a plate. Rest for 5 minutes before serving.

Mini Turkey Meatloaves with Carrot

Prep time: 6 minutes, Cook time: 22 minutes, Serves 4

15 g minced onion   40 g grated carrot   1 tsp. dried marjoram   1 egg white
2 garlic cloves, minced   2 tsps. olive oil   350 g turkey mince breast
2 tbsps. ground almonds

1. In a medium bowl, stir together the onion, carrot, garlic, almonds, olive oil, marjoram, and egg white.
2. Add the turkey mince. With your hands, gently but thoroughly mix until combined.
3. Double 16 foil muffin cup liners to make 8 cups. Divide the turkey mixture evenly among the liners.
4. Install a crisper plate in both baskets. Place 4 cups in a single layer in each basket.
5. Select Zone 1, select AIR FRY, set temperature to 200℃, and set time to 22 minutes. Select MATCH COOK to match Zone 2 settings to Zone 1. Select START/PAUSE to begin cooking.
6. When cooking is complete, transfer the turkey meatloaves to a plate. Serve warm.

Roasted Chicken with Potatoes

Prep time: 15 minutes, Cook time: 45 minutes, Serves 2

1 whole chicken   250 g small potatoes
Salt and black pepper, as required   1 tbsp. olive oil

1. Season the chicken and potatoes with salt and black pepper and drizzle with olive oil.
2. Install a crisper plate in both baskets. Place chicken in the Zone 1 basket, then insert basket in unit. Place potatoes in the Zone 2 basket, then insert basket in unit.
3. Select Zone 1, select ROAST, set temperature to 200℃, and set time to 45 minutes. Select Zone 2, select AIR FRY, set temperature to 200℃, and set time to 30 minutes. Select SMART FINISH. Press the START/PAUSE button to begin cooking.
4. When the Zone 1 and Zone 2 times reach 15 minutes, press START/PAUSE and remove baskets from unit. In Zone 1, flip the chicken over. In Zone 2, shake for 10 seconds. Reinsert baskets in unit and press START/PAUSE to resume cooking.
5. When cooking is complete, serve chicken with potatoes.

Crispy Herbed Turkey Breast

Prep time: 5 minutes, Cook time: 30 minutes, Serves 2

½ tbsp. fresh rosemary, chopped

2 turkey breasts

1 tbsp. ginger, minced

Salt and black pepper, to taste

½ tbsp. fresh parsley, chopped

1 garlic clove, minced

1 tsp. five spice powder

1. Mix garlic, herbs, five spice powder, salt and black pepper in a bowl.
2. Brush the turkey breasts generously with garlic mixture.
3. Install a crisper plate in a basket. Place turkey breasts in the basket, then insert basket in unit.
4. Select Zone 1, select ROAST, set temperature to 200°C and set time to 30 minutes. Press the START/PAUSE button to begin cooking.
5. With 15 minutes remaining, press START/PAUSE to pause the unit. Remove the basket from unit and flip the turkey breasts over. Reinsert basket in unit and press START/PAUSE to resume cooking.
6. When cooking is complete, remove basket from unit. Transfer turkey breasts to a plate. Serve warm.

Appetizing Chicken

Prep time: 30 minutes, Cook time: 18 minutes, Serves 2

350 g chicken pieces 1 lemon, cut into wedges

1 tbsp. soy sauce

1 tbsp. oyster sauce

1 tbsp. fresh rosemary, chopped

1 tsp. ginger, minced

½ tbsp. olive oil

3 tbsps. coconut sugar

1. Mix chicken, ginger, soy sauce and olive oil in a bowl.
2. Marinate and refrigerate for about 30 minutes.
3. Install a crisper plate in a basket. Place chicken in the basket, then insert basket in unit.
4. Select Zone 1, select AIR FRY, set temperature to 200°C, and set time to 18 minutes. Press the START/PAUSE button to begin cooking.
5. Meanwhile, mix the remaining ingredients in a small bowl.
6. With 10 minutes remaining, press START/PAUSE to pause the unit. Remove the basket from unit. Spread the sauce over the chicken. Squeeze juice from lemon wedges over chicken and top with the wedges. Reinsert basket in unit and press START/PAUSE to resume cooking.
7. When cooking is complete, remove basket from unit. Transfer chicken to a plate. Serve warm.

Chicken with Apple

Prep time: 10 minutes, Cook time: 20 minutes, Serves 8

1 shallot, thinly sliced   1 tsp. fresh thyme, minced
2 (120 g) boneless, skinless chicken thighs, sliced into chunks
1 large apple, cored and cubed
1 tbsp. fresh ginger, finely grated
120 ml apple cider   2 tbsps. maple syrup
Salt and black pepper, as required

1. Preheat the Air fryer to 200ºC and grease an Air fryer basket.
2. Mix the shallot, ginger, thyme, apple cider, maple syrup, salt, and black pepper in a bowl.
3. Coat the chicken generously with the marinade and refrigerate to marinate for about 8 hours.
4. Install a crisper plate in both baskets. Place chicken pieces in the Zone 1 basket, then insert basket in unit. Place cubed apples in the Zone 2 basket, then insert basket in unit.
5. Select Zone 1, select AIR FRY, set temperature to 200℃, and set time to 20 minutes. Select Zone 2, select AIR FRY, set temperature to 200℃, and set time to 15 minutes. Select SMART FINISH. Press the START/PAUSE button to begin cooking.
6. When the Zone 1 and Zone 2 times reach 10 minutes, press START/PAUSE and remove baskets from unit. In Zone 1, flip the chicken pieces over. In Zone 2, shake for 10 seconds. Reinsert baskets in unit and press START/PAUSE to resume cooking.
7. When cooking is complete, serve chicken with apples.

Succulent Duck Breast with Balsamic Vinaigrette

Prep time: 15 minutes, Cook time: 20 minutes, Serves 2

1 tbsp. fresh thyme, chopped   1 tbsp. olive oil   1 tsp. mustard
1 (150 g) duck breast   250 ml beer   1 tbsp. balsamic vinegar
4 cherry tomatoes   50 g black olives   Salt and freshly ground black pepper, to taste

1. Mix olive oil, mustard, thyme, beer, salt and black pepper in a bowl.
2. Add duck breast and coat generously with marinade.
3. Cover the duck breast with foil paper and refrigerate for about 4 hours.
4. Install a crisper plate in both baskets. Place duck breast in the Zone 1 basket, then insert basket in unit. Place tomatoes in the Zone 2 basket, then insert basket in unit.
5. Select Zone 1, select ROAST, set temperature to 200℃, and set time to 25 minutes. Select Zone 2, select ROAST, set temperature to 200℃, and set time to 15 minutes. Select SMART FINISH. Press the START/PAUSE button to begin cooking.
6. When the Zone 1 and 2 times reach 10 minutes, press START/PAUSE to pause the unit. Remove the baskets from unit and flip the duck breast and cherry tomatoes over. Reinsert baskets in unit and press START/PAUSE to resume cooking.
7. When cooking is complete, transfer the duck and tomatoes to a plate. Drizzle with vinegar and serve topped with olives.

Chinese Chicken Drumsticks

Prep time: 15 minutes, Cook time: 22 minutes, Serves 4

4 (200 g) chicken drumsticks

1 tbsp. oyster sauce   1 tsp. light soy sauce

½ tsp. sesame oil   100 g corn flour

1 tsp. Chinese five spice powder

Salt and white pepper, as required

1. Mix the sauces, oil, five spice powder, salt, and black pepper in a bowl.
2. Rub the chicken drumsticks with marinade and refrigerate for about 40 minutes.
3. Install a crisper plate in a basket. Place drumsticks in the basket, then insert basket in unit.
4. Select Zone 1, select AIR FRY, set temperature to 200℃, and set time to 22 minutes. Press the START/PAUSE button to begin cooking.
5. With 10 minutes remaining, press START/PAUSE to pause the unit. Remove the basket from unit and flip the drumsticks over. Reinsert basket in unit and press START/PAUSE to resume cooking.
6. When cooking is complete, remove basket from unit. Transfer drumsticks to a plate. Serve warm.

Mouthwatering Turkey Roll

Prep time: 20 minutes, Cook time: 40 minutes, Serves 4

500 g turkey breast fillet, deep slit cut lengthwise with knife

3 tbsps. fresh parsley, chopped finely

1 small red onion, chopped finely

1 garlic clove, crushed   ½ tsp. red chilli powder

1½ tsps. ground cumin   1 tsp. ground cinnamon

Salt, to taste   2 tbsps. olive oil

1. Mix garlic, parsley, onion, spices and olive oil in a bowl.
2. Coat the open side of fillet with onion mixture and roll the fillet tightly.
3. Coat the outer side of roll with remaining spice mixture.
4. Install a crisper plate in a basket. Place the turkey breast in the basket, then insert basket in unit.
5. Select Zone 1, select ROAST, set temperature to 200℃, and set time to 40 minutes. Press the START/PAUSE button to begin cooking.
6. With 20 minutes remaining, press START/PAUSE to pause the unit. Remove the basket from unit and flip the turkey breast over. Reinsert basket in unit and press START/PAUSE to resume cooking.
7. When cooking is complete, remove basket from unit. Transfer turkey breast to a plate. Serve warm.

Roasted Cajun Turkey

Prep time: 10 minutes, Cook time: 30 minutes, Serves 4

900 g turkey thighs, skinless and boneless
1 red onion, sliced   2 bell peppers, sliced
1 habanero pepper, minced   1 carrot, sliced

1 tbsp. Cajun seasoning mix
1 tbsp. fish sauce   500 ml chicken broth
Nonstick cooking spray

1. Add the turkey thighs, onion, peppers, and carrot with Cajun seasoning, fish sauce and chicken broth and mix well. Lightly spray with the cooking spray.
2. Install a crisper plate in both baskets. Place turkey thigh in the Zone 1 basket, then insert basket in unit. Place vegetables in the Zone 2 basket, then insert basket in unit.
3. Select Zone 1, select ROAST, set temperature to 200°C, and set time to 30 minutes. Select Zone 2, select AIR FRY, set temperature to 200°C, and set time to 20 minutes. Select SMART FINISH. Press the START/PAUSE button to begin cooking.
4. When the Zone 1 and Zone 2 times reach 10 minutes, press START/PAUSE and remove baskets from unit. In Zone 1, flip the turkey thigh. In Zone 2, shake for 10 seconds. Reinsert baskets in unit and press START/PAUSE to resume cooking.
5. When cooking is complete, serve turkey thigh with vegetables.

Deliciously Crisp Chicken

Prep time: 10 minutes, Cook time: 28 minutes, Serves 4

1 egg, beaten   60 g bread crumbs
8 skinless, boneless chicken tenderloins

2 tbsps. vegetable oil

1. Whisk the egg in a shallow dish and mix vegetable oil and breadcrumbs in another shallow dish.
2. Dip the chicken tenderloins in egg and then coat in the breadcrumb mixture.
3. Install a crisper plate in both baskets. Place 4 chicken tenderloins in a single layer in each basket.
4. Select Zone 1, select ROAST, set temperature to 200°C, and set time to 28 minutes. Select MATCH COOK to match Zone 2 settings to Zone 1. Select START/PAUSE to begin cooking.
5. When the Zone 1 and 2 times reach 12 minutes, press START/PAUSE to pause the unit. Remove the baskets from unit and flip the chicken tenderloins over. Reinsert baskets in unit and press START/PAUSE to resume cooking.
6. When cooking is complete, transfer chicken tenderloins to a plate. Serve warm.

Air-Fried Chicken Wings

Prep time: 5 minutes, Cook time: 22 minutes, Serves 6

900 g chicken wings, tips removed ⅛ tsp. salt

1. Season the wings with salt.
2. Install a crisper plate in a basket. Place the wings in the basket, then insert basket in unit.
3. Select Zone 1, select AIR FRY, set temperature to 200℃, and set time to 22 minutes. Press the START/PAUSE button to begin cooking.
4. With 10 minutes remaining, press START/PAUSE to pause the unit. Remove the basket from unit and flip the wings over. Reinsert basket in unit and press START/PAUSE to resume cooking.
5. When cooking is complete, remove basket from unit. Transfer the wings to a plate. Serve warm.

Gingered Chicken Drumsticks

Prep time: 10 minutes, Cook time: 22 minutes, Serves 3

60 ml full-fat coconut milk
3 (200 g) chicken drumsticks 2
tsps. fresh ginger, minced

2 tsps. galangal, minced
2 tsps. ground turmeric   Salt, to taste

1. Mix the coconut milk, galangal, ginger, and spices in a bowl.
2. Add the chicken drumsticks and coat generously with the marinade.
3. Refrigerate to marinate for at least 8 hours.
4. Install a crisper plate in a basket. Place chicken drumsticks in the basket, then insert basket in unit.
5. Select Zone 1, select AIR FRY, set temperature to 200℃, and set time to 22 minutes. Press the START/PAUSE button to begin cooking.
6. With 10 minutes remaining, press START/PAUSE to pause the unit. Remove the basket from unit and flip the chicken drumsticks over. Reinsert basket in unit and press START/PAUSE to resume cooking.
7. When cooking is complete, remove basket from unit. Transfer chicken drumsticks to a plate. Serve warm.

CHAPTER 3 VEGETABLES

Cauliflower Salad

Prep time: 20 minutes, Cook time: 20 minutes, Serves 4

40 g golden raisins   250 ml boiling water
1 head cauliflower, cut into small florets
40 g pecans, toasted and chopped
2 tbsps. fresh mint leaves, chopped

60 ml olive oil   1 tbsp. curry powder
Salt, to taste
For the Dressing:
250g mayonnaise   2 tbsps. coconut sugar
1 tbsp. fresh lemon juice

1. Mix the cauliflower, pecans, curry powder, salt, and olive oil in a bowl and toss to coat well.
2. Install a crisper plate in a basket. Place cauliflower florets in the basket, then insert basket in unit.
3. Select Zone 1, select ROAST, set temperature to 200℃, and set time to 20 minutes. Press the START/PAUSE button to begin cooking.
4. Meanwhile, add the raisins in boiling water in a bowl for about 20 minutes.
5. With 10 minutes remaining, press START/PAUSE to pause the unit. Remove the basket from unit and flip the cauliflower florets over. Reinsert basket in unit and press START/PAUSE to resume cooking.
6. When cooking is complete, remove basket from unit. Transfer cauliflower florets to a plate. Drain the raisins well and mix with the cauliflower florets.
7. Mix all the ingredients for dressing in a bowl and pour over the salad.
8. Toss to coat well and serve immediately.

Aubergine Salad

Prep time: 15 minutes, Cook time: 15 minutes, Serves 2

1 aubergine, cut into 1 cm-thick slices crosswise
1 avocado, peeled, pitted and chopped   2 tbsps. canola oil
Salt and ground black pepper, as required   1 tsp. fresh lemon juice

For the Dressing:

1 tbsp. extra-virgin olive oil   1 tsp. Dijon mustard
1 tbsp. red wine vinegar   1 tbsp. honey
1 tbsp. fresh oregano leaves, chopped   1 tsp. fresh lemon zest, grated
Salt and ground black pepper, as required

1. Mix aubergine, oil, salt, and black pepper in a bowl and toss to coat well.
2. Install a crisper plate in a basket. Place Aubergines pieces in the basket, then insert basket in unit.
3. Select Zone 1, select AIR FRY, set temperature to 200℃, and set time to 15 minutes. Press the START/PAUSE button to begin cooking.
4. With 8 minutes remaining, press START/PAUSE to pause the unit. Remove the basket from unit and flip the Aubergines pieces over. Reinsert basket in unit and press START/PAUSE to resume cooking.
5. When cooking is complete, remove basket from unit. Transfer Aubergines to a plate and keep aside to cool.
6. Add avocado and lemon juice and mix well.
7. Mix all the ingredients for dressing in a bowl and pour over the salad.
8. Toss to coat well and serve immediately.

Rice and Beans Stuffed Bell Peppers

Prep time: 15 minutes, Cook time: 16 minutes, Serves 5

1 (450 g) can diced tomatoes with juice
1 (450 g) can red kidney beans, rinsed and drained
150 g cooked rice
5 large bell peppers, tops removed and seeded
120 g mozzarella cheese, shredded   1½ tsps. Italian seasoning

1. Mix rice, tomatoes with juice, beans, and Italian seasoning in a bowl.
2. Halve the bell peppers and stuff the rice mixture in each bell pepper half.
3. Install a crisper plate in both baskets. Place half of the stuffed bell peppers in a single layer in each basket.
4. Select Zone 1, select BAKE, set temperature to 200°C and set time to 16 minutes. Select MATCH COOK to match Zone 2 settings to Zone 1. Select START/PAUSE to begin cooking.
5. When the Zone 1 and 2 times reach 8 minutes, press START/PAUSE to pause the unit. Remove the baskets from unit and top the bell peppers with mozzarella cheese. Reinsert baskets in unit and press START/PAUSE to resume cooking.
6. When cooking is complete, transfer bell peppers to a plate. Serve warm.

Tofu with Orange Sauce

Prep time: 20 minutes, Cook time: 12 minutes, Serves 4

500 g extra-firm tofu, pressed and cubed   1 tbsp. honey   1 tsp. orange zest, grated
120 ml water   4 tsps. cornflour, divided   1 tsp. garlic, minced
2 spring onions (green part), chopped   1 tsp. fresh ginger, minced
1 tbsp. tamari   75 ml fresh orange juice   ¼ tsp. red pepper flakes, crushed

1. Mix the tofu, cornflour, and tamari in a bowl and toss to coat well.
2. Install a crisper plate in both baskets. Place half of the tofu pieces in a single layer in each basket.
3. Select Zone 1, select AIR FRY, set temperature to 200°C, and set time to 12 minutes. Select MATCH COOK to match Zone 2 settings to Zone 1. Select START/PAUSE to begin cooking.
4. When the Zone 1 and 2 times reach 6 minutes, press START/PAUSE to pause the unit. Remove the baskets from unit and tofu pieces over. Reinsert baskets in unit and press START/PAUSE to resume cooking.
5. When cooking is complete, transfer tofu pieces to a plate.
6. Put all the ingredients except spring onions in a small pan over medium-high heat and bring to a boil.
7. Pour this sauce over the tofu and garnish with spring onions to serve.

Stuffed Pumpkin

Prep time: 20 minutes, Cook time: 35 minutes, Serves 4

2 tomatoes, chopped   1 beetroot, chopped

1 bell pepper, chopped

60g green beans, shelled

½ of butternut pumpkin, seeded

2 garlic cloves, minced

2 tsps. mixed dried herbs

Salt and black pepper, to taste

1. Mix all the ingredients in a bowl except pumpkin and toss to coat well.
2. Install a crisper plate in a basket. Stuff the vegetable mixture into the pumpkin and place in the basket, then insert basket in unit.
3. Select Zone 1, select ROAST, set temperature to 180°C, and set time to 35 minutes. Press the START/PAUSE button to begin cooking.
4. When cooking is complete, remove basket from unit. Transfer pumpkin to a plate and keep aside to slightly cool. Serve warm.

Bell Peppers Cups

Prep time: 10 minutes, Cook time: 15 minutes, Serves 4

8 mini red bell peppers, tops and seeds removed

1 tsp. fresh parsley, chopped

110 g feta cheese, crumbled

½ tbsp. olive oil

Freshly ground black pepper, to taste

1. Mix feta cheese, parsley, olive oil and black pepper in a bowl.
2. Stuff the bell peppers with feta cheese mixture.
3. Install a crisper plate in both baskets. Place 4 bell peppers in a single layer in each basket.
4. Select Zone 1, select AIR FRY, set temperature to 200°C, and set time to 15 minutes. Select MATCH COOK to match Zone 2 settings to Zone 1. Select START/PAUSE to begin cooking.
5. When cooking is complete, transfer bell peppers to a plate. Serve warm.

Family Favourite Potatoes

Prep time: 10 minutes, Cook time: 22 minutes, Serves 4

800 g waxy potatoes, cubed and boiled

120 g Greek yoghurt

2 tbsps. olive oil, divided

1 tbsp. paprika, divided

Salt and black pepper, to taste

1. Mix 1 tbsp. olive oil, ⅓ tbsp. of paprika, black pepper and potatoes in a bowl and toss to coat well.
2. Install a crisper plate in a basket. Place potatoes in the basket, then insert basket in unit.
3. Select Zone 1, select AIR FRY, set temperature to 200°C, and set time to 22 minutes. Press the START/PAUSE button to begin cooking.
4. With 11 minutes remaining, press START/PAUSE to pause the unit. Remove the basket from unit and shake for 10 seconds. Reinsert basket in unit and press START/PAUSE to resume cooking.
5. When cooking is complete, remove basket from unit. Transfer potatoes to a plate. Mix yoghurt, remaining oil, salt and black pepper in a bowl and serve with potatoes.

Chewy Glazed Parsnips

Prep time: 10 minutes, Cook time: 35 minutes, Serves 6

900 g parsnips, peeled and cut into 2 cm chunks
1 tbsp. butter, melted   2 tbsps. maple syrup
1 tbsp. dried parsley flakes, crushed
¼ tsp. red pepper flakes, crushed

1. Mix parsnips and butter in a bowl and toss to coat well.
2. Install a crisper plate in both baskets. Place half of the parsnips in each basket.
3. Select Zone 1, select AIR FRY, set temperature to 200°C and set time to 35 minutes. Select MATCH COOK to match Zone 2 settings to Zone 1. Select START/PAUSE to begin cooking.
4. When the Zone 1 and 2 times reach 15 minutes, press START/PAUSE to pause the unit. Remove the baskets from unit and shake for 10 seconds. Reinsert baskets in unit and press START/PAUSE to resume cooking.
5. Meanwhile, mix remaining ingredients in a large bowl.
6. When the Zone 1 and 2 times reach 5 minutes, press START/PAUSE to pause the unit. Remove the baskets from unit and spread the mixture over parsnips. Reinsert baskets in unit and press START/PAUSE to resume cooking.
7. When cooking is complete, transfer the parsnips to a plate. Serve warm.

Veggie Stuffed Bell Peppers

Prep time: 20 minutes, Cook time: 25 minutes, Serves 6

6 large bell peppers, tops and seeds removed
1 carrot, peeled and finely chopped
1 potato, peeled and finely chopped
70 g fresh peas, shelled

30 g cheddar cheese, grated
2 garlic cloves, minced
Salt and black pepper, to taste

1. Mix vegetables, garlic, salt and black pepper in a bowl.
2. Stuff the vegetable mixture in each bell pepper.
3. Install a crisper plate in both baskets. Place half of bell peppers in a single layer in each basket.
4. Select Zone 1, select AIR FRY, set temperature to 200°C, and set time to 25 minutes. Select MATCH COOK to match Zone 2 settings to Zone 1. Select START/PAUSE to begin cooking.
5. When the Zone 1 and 2 times reach 5 minutes, press START/PAUSE to pause the unit. Remove the baskets from unit and top with cheddar cheese. Reinsert baskets in unit and press START/PAUSE to resume cooking.
6. When cooking is complete, transfer bell peppers to a plate. Serve warm.

Courgette Salad

Prep time: 15 minutes, Cook time: 28 minutes, Serves 4

500 g courgette, cut into rounds

150 g fresh spinach, chopped

50 g feta cheese, crumbled

2 tbsps. olive oil   1 tsp. garlic powder

Salt and black pepper, as required

2 tbsps. fresh lemon juice

1. Mix the courgette, oil, garlic powder, salt, and black pepper in a bowl and toss to coat well.
2. Install a crisper plate in a basket. Place courgette slices in the basket, then insert basket in unit.
3. Select Zone 1, select AIR FRY, set temperature to 200℃, and set time to 28 minutes. Press the START/PAUSE button to begin cooking.
4. With 14 minutes remaining, press START/PAUSE to pause the unit. Remove the basket from unit and flip the courgette slices over. Reinsert basket in unit and press START/PAUSE to resume cooking.
5. When cooking is complete, remove basket from unit. Transfer courgette slices to a plate and keep aside to cool.
6. Add spinach, feta cheese, lemon juice, a little bit of salt and black pepper and mix well. Toss to coat well and serve immediately.

Garden Fresh Green Beans

Prep time: 10 minutes, Cook time: 12 minutes, Serves 4

cooking spray   ¼ tsp. garlic powder

500 g green beans, washed and trimmed

1 tsp. butter, melted   1 tbsp. fresh lemon juice

Salt and freshly ground pepper, to taste

1. Put all the ingredients in a large bowl.
2. Install a crisper plate in a basket. Place green beans in the basket and spray with cooking spray, then insert basket in unit.
3. Select Zone 1, select AIR FRY, set temperature to 200℃, and set time to 12 minutes. Press the START/PAUSE button to begin cooking.
4. With 6 minutes remaining, press START/PAUSE to pause the unit. Remove the basket from unit and flip the green beans over. Reinsert basket in unit and press START/PAUSE to resume cooking.
5. When cooking is complete, remove basket from unit. Transfer green beans to a plate. Serve warm.

Broccoli with Cauliflower

Prep time: 15 minutes, Cook time: 20 minutes, Serves 4

100 g broccoli, cut into 2 cm pieces

1 tbsp. olive oil

100 g cauliflower, cut into 2 cm pieces

Salt, as required

1. Mix the vegetables, olive oil, and salt in a bowl and toss to coat well.
2. Install a crisper plate in both baskets. Place broccoli in the Zone 1 basket, then insert basket in unit. Place cauliflower in the Zone 2 basket, then insert basket in unit.
3. Select Zone 1, select ROAST, set temperature to 200℃, and set time to 15 minutes. Select Zone 2, select ROAST, set temperature to 200℃, and set time to 20 minutes. Select SMART FINISH. Press the START/PAUSE button to begin cooking.
4. When the Zone 1 and 2 times reach 8 minutes, press START/PAUSE to pause the unit. Remove the baskets from unit and shake for 10 seconds. Reinsert baskets in unit and press START/PAUSE to resume cooking.
5. When cooking is complete, serve immediately.

Green Beans and Mushroom

Prep time: 15 minutes, Cook time: 15 minutes, Serves 6

680 g fresh green beans, trimmed

250 g fresh button mushrooms, sliced

20 g French fried onions   3 tbsps. olive oil

2 tbsps. fresh lemon juice   1 tsp. ground sage

1 tsp. garlic powder   1 tsp. onion powder

Salt and black pepper, to taste

1. Mix the green beans, mushrooms, oil, lemon juice, sage, and spices in a bowl and toss to coat well.

2. Install a crisper plate in both baskets. Place green beans in the Zone 1 basket, then insert basket in unit. Place mushrooms in the Zone 2 basket, then insert basket in unit.

3. Select Zone 1, select AIR FRY, set temperature to 200℃, and set time to 15 minutes. Select Zone 2, select AIR FRY, set temperature to 200℃, and set time to 12 minutes. Select SMART FINISH. Press the START/PAUSE button to begin cooking.

4. When the Zone 1 and 2 times reach 6 minutes, press START/PAUSE to pause the unit. Remove the baskets from unit and shake for 10 seconds. Reinsert baskets in unit and press START/PAUSE to resume cooking.

5. When cooking is complete, serve green beans with mushrooms.

Ultra-Crispy Tofu

Prep time: 15 minutes, Cook time: 18 minutes, Serves 4

cooking spray   1 tsp. chicken bouillon granules

350 g extra-firm tofu, drained and cubed into 2 cm size

1 tsp. butter   2 tbsps. low-sodium soy sauce

2 tbsps. fish sauce 1 tsp. sesame oil

1. Mix soy sauce, fish sauce, sesame oil and chicken granules in a bowl and toss to coat well.

2. Stir in the tofu cubes and mix until well combined. Keep aside to marinate for about 30 minutes.

3. Install a crisper plate in a basket. Place tofu cubes in the basket and spray with cooking spray, then insert basket in unit.

4. Select Zone 1, select AIR FRY, set temperature to 200°C and set time to 18 minutes. Press the START/PAUSE button to begin cooking.

5. With 8 minutes remaining, press START/PAUSE to pause the unit. Remove the basket from unit and flip the tofu cubes over. Reinsert basket in unit and press START/PAUSE to resume cooking.

6. When cooking is complete, remove basket from unit. Transfer tofu cubes to a plate. Serve warm.

CHAPTER 4 FISH AND SEAFOOD

Juicy Salmon and Asparagus

Prep time: 5 minutes, Cook time: 20 minutes, Serves 2

2 salmon fillets	4 asparagus stalks	125 ml champagne
125 ml white sauce	Salt and black pepper, to taste	1 tsp. olive oil

1. Mix all the ingredients in a bowl.
2. Install a crisper plate in both baskets. Place salmon fillets in the Zone 1 basket, then insert basket in unit. Place asparagus stalks in the Zone 2 basket, then insert basket in unit.
3. Select Zone 1, select AIR FRY, set temperature to 200℃, and set time to 15 minutes. Select Zone 2, select ROAST, set temperature to 200℃, and set time to 20 minutes. Select SMART FINISH. Press the START/PAUSE button to begin cooking.
4. When the Zone 1 and 2 times reach 8 minutes, press START/PAUSE to pause the unit. Remove the baskets from unit and flip the salmon and asparagus. Reinsert baskets in unit and press START/PAUSE to resume cooking.
5. When cooking is complete, serve salmon with asparagus.

Honey Glazed Salmon

Prep time: 10 minutes, Cook time: 10 minutes, Serves 2

1 tsp. water	2 (100 g) salmon fillets	3 tsps. rice wine vinegar
80 ml soy sauce	80 ml honey	

1. Mix all the ingredients in a small bowl except salmon.
2. Reserve half of the mixture in a small bowl and coat the salmon in remaining mixture. Refrigerate, covered for about 2 hours.
3. Install a crisper plate in a basket. Place salmon in the basket, then insert basket in unit.
4. Select Zone 1, select AIR FRY, set temperature to 200℃, and set time to 9 minutes. Press the START/PAUSE button to begin cooking.
5. Place the reserved marinade in a small pan and cook for about 1 minute.
6. When cooking is complete, remove basket from unit. Transfer salmon to a plate. Serve salmon with marinade sauce and enjoy.

Cod with Shrimps and Pasta

Prep time: 20 minutes, Cook time: 25 minutes, Serves 4

400 g pasta	4 (100 g) cod steaks	4 tbsps. pesto, divided 2 tbsps. olive oil
8 large shrimps, peeled and deveined		2 tbsps. fresh lemon juice
2 tbsps. fresh parsley, chopped		

1. Cook pasta in a large pan of salted water for about 10 minutes.
2. Meanwhile, spread pesto over cod steaks and drizzle evenly with olive oil.
3. Sprinkle shrimps with lemon juice and parsley.
4. Install a crisper plate in both baskets. Place cod steaks in the Zone 1 basket, then insert basket in unit. Place shrimps in the Zone 2 basket, then insert basket in unit.
5. Select Zone 1, select AIR FRY, set temperature to 200℃, and set time to 15 minutes. Select Zone 2, select AIR FRY, set temperature to 200℃, and set time to 13 minutes. Select SMART FINISH. Press the START/PAUSE button to begin cooking.
6. When cooking is complete, serve the cod with shrimps and pasta.

Homemade Fish Fingers

Prep time: 15 minutes, Cook time: 15 minutes, Serves 4

4 fish fillets	60 g whole-wheat flour	180 g whole-wheat panko bread crumbs
1 tsp. seasoned salt	2 eggs	½ tbsp. dried parsley flakes Cooking spray

1. Cut the fish fillets lengthwise into "sticks."
2. In a shallow bowl, mix the whole-wheat flour and seasoned salt.
3. In a small bowl, whisk the eggs with 1 tsp. of water.
4. In another shallow bowl, mix the panko bread crumbs and parsley flakes.
5. Coat each fish stick in the seasoned flour, then in the egg mixture, and dredge them in the panko bread crumbs.
6. Install a crisper plate in both baskets. Place half of fish fingers in a single layer in each basket.
7. Select Zone 1, select AIR FRY, set temperature to 200℃, and set time to 15 minutes. Select MATCH COOK to match Zone 2 settings to Zone 1. Select START/PAUSE to begin cooking.
8. When the Zone 1 and 2 times reach 8 minutes, press START/PAUSE to pause the unit. Remove the baskets from unit and flip the fish sticks over. Lightly spray with the cooking spray. Reinsert baskets in unit and press START/PAUSE to resume cooking.
9. When cooking is complete, transfer fish fingers to a plate. Serve warm.

Air Fried Spring Rolls

Prep time: 10 minutes, Cook time: 18 minutes, Serves 4

2 tsps. minced garlic   200 g inely sliced cabbage

100 g matchstick cut carrots

2 (100 g) cans tiny shrimp, drained   4 tsps. soy sauce

Salt and freshly ground black pepper, to taste

16 square spring roll wrappers   Cooking spray

1. Spray a medium sauté pan with cooking spray.
2. Add the garlic to the sauté pan and cook over medium heat until fragrant, 30 to 45 seconds. Add the cabbage and carrots and sauté until the vegetables are slightly tender, about 5 minutes.
3. Add the shrimp and soy sauce and season with salt and pepper, then stir to combine. Sauté until the moisture has evaporated, 2 more minutes. Set aside to cool.
4. Place a spring roll wrapper on a work surface so it looks like a diamond. Place 1 tbsp. of the shrimp mixture on the lower end of the wrapper.
5. Roll the wrapper away from you halfway, then fold in the right and left sides, like an envelope. Continue to roll to the very end, using a little water to seal the edge. Repeat with the remaining wrappers and filling.
6. Install a crisper plate in both baskets. Place half of spring rolls in a single layer in each basket. Lightly spray with cooking spray.
7. Select Zone 1, select AIR FRY, set temperature to 190℃, and set time to 10 minutes. Select MATCH COOK to match Zone 2 settings to Zone 1. Select START/PAUSE to begin cooking.
8. When cooking is complete, transfer spring rolls to a plate. Let cool for 5 minutes before serving.

Cajun-Style Salmon Burgers

Prep time: 10 minutes, Cook time: 10 to 15 minutes, Serves 4

4 (150-g) cans pink salmon in water, any skin and   4 tbsps. light mayonnaise

bones removed, drained   2 tsps. Cajun seasoning

2 eggs, beaten   2 tsps. dry mustard   4 whole-wheat buns

120 g whole-wheat bread crumbs   Cooking spray

1. In a medium bowl, mix the salmon, egg, bread crumbs, mayonnaise, Cajun seasoning, and dry mustard. Cover with plastic wrap and refrigerate for 30 minutes.
2. Shape the mixture into four 1 cm-thick patties about the same size as the buns.
3. Install a crisper plate in both baskets. Place 2 salmon patties in a single layer in each basket. Lightly spray the tops with cooking spray.
4. Select Zone 1, select AIR FRY, set temperature to 200℃, and set time to 13 minutes. Select MATCH COOK to match Zone 2 settings to Zone 1. Select START/PAUSE to begin cooking.
5. When the Zone 1 and 2 times reach 8 minutes, press START/PAUSE to pause the unit. Remove the baskets from unit and flip the patties over. Lightly spray with cooking spray. Reinsert baskets in unit and press START/PAUSE to resume cooking.
6. When cooking is complete, transfer patties to a plate. Serve on whole-wheat buns.

Salmon with Broccoli

Prep time: 15 minutes, Cook time: 15 minutes, Serves 2

100 g small broccoli florets
¼ tsp. cornflour
2 (180 g) salmon fillets, skin-on
1 spring onion, thinly sliced
2 tbsps. vegetable oil, divided

Salt and black pepper, as required
1 (1 cm) piece fresh ginger, grated
1 tbsp. soy sauce   1 tsp. rice vinegar
1 tsp. light brown sugar

1. Mix the broccoli, 1 tbsp. of vegetable oil, salt, and black pepper.
2. Combine ginger, soy sauce, rice vinegar, sugar and cornflour in another bowl.
3. Rub the salmon fillets evenly with remaining olive oil and the ginger mixture.
4. Install a crisper plate in both baskets. Place broccoli florets in the Zone 1 basket, then insert basket in unit. Place salmon fillets in the Zone 2 basket, then insert basket in unit.
5. Select Zone 1, select AIR FRY, set temperature to 200℃, and set time to 15 minutes. Select MATCH COOK to match Zone 2 settings to Zone 1. Press the START/PAUSE button to begin cooking.
6. When the Zone 1 and 2 times reach 8 minutes, press START/PAUSE to pause the unit. Remove the baskets from unit. Shake the broccoli for 10 seconds and flip the salmon over. Reinsert baskets in unit and press START/PAUSE to resume cooking.
7. When cooking is complete, serve salmon with broccoli.

Chinese Style Cod

Prep time: 20 minutes, Cook time: 15 minutes, Serves 2

2 (200 g) cod fillets   250 ml water
2 spring onions (green part), sliced
40 g fresh coriander, chopped
Salt and black pepper, to taste
¼ tsp. sesame oil

5 little squares rock sugar
5 tbsps. light soy sauce
1 tsp. dark soy sauce   3 tbsps. olive oil
5 ginger slices

1. Season each cod fillet with salt and black pepper and drizzle with sesame oil.
2. Install a crisper plate in a basket. Place cod fillets in the basket, then insert basket in unit.
3. Select Zone 1, select AIR FRY, set temperature to 200℃, and set time to 12 minutes. Press the START/PAUSE button to begin cooking.
4. Meanwhile, bring water to boil and add rock sugar and both soy sauces. Cook until sugar is dissolved, continuously stirring and keep aside.
5. When cooking is complete, remove basket from unit. Transfer cod fillets to a plate and top each fillet with coriander and spring onions.
6. Heat olive oil over medium heat in a small frying pan and add ginger slices.
7. Sauté for about 3 minutes and discard the ginger slices.
8. Drizzle the hot oil over cod fillets and top with the sauce mixture to serve.

Quick and Easy Prawns

Prep time: 10 minutes, Cook time: 7 minutes, Serves 2

250 g tiger prawns

½ tsp. old bay seasoning

¼ tsp. cayenne pepper

1 tbsp. olive oil

¼ tsp. smoked paprika

Salt, to taste

1. Mix all the ingredients in a large bowl until well combined.
2. Install a crisper plate in a basket. Place prawns in the basket, then insert basket in unit.
3. Select Zone 1, select AIR FRY, set temperature to 200°C, and set time to 7 minutes. Press the START/PAUSE button to begin cooking.
4. When cooking is complete, remove basket from unit. Transfer prawns to a plate. Serve warm.

Spicy Cod

Prep time: 10 minutes, Cook time: 12 minutes, Serves 2

2 (200 g) (40 cm thick) cod illets

1 tsp. smoked paprika   1 tsp. cayenne pepper

1 tsp. onion powder   1 tsp. garlic powder

Salt and ground black pepper, as required

2 tsps. olive oil

1. Drizzle the salmon fillets with olive oil and rub with the all the spices.
2. Install a crisper plate in a basket. Place salmon fillets in the basket, then insert basket in unit.
3. Select Zone 1, select ROAST, set temperature to 200°C, and set time to 12 minutes. Press the START/PAUSE button to begin cooking.
4. When cooking is complete, remove basket from unit. Transfer salmon fillets to a plate. Serve warm.

Cheesy Prawns

Prep time: 20 minutes, Cook time: 12 minutes, Serves 4

60 g Parmesan cheese, grated

1 kg Prawns, peeled and deveined

4 garlic cloves, minced   2 tbsps. olive oil

1 tsp. dried basil   ½ tsp. dried oregano

1 tsp. onion powder   2 tbsps. fresh lemon juice

½ tsp. red pepper flakes, crushed

Ground black pepper, as required

1. Mix Parmesan cheese, garlic, olive oil, herbs, and spices in a large bowl and stir in the prawns.
2. Install a crisper plate in both baskets. Place half of the prawns in a single layer in each basket.
3. Select Zone 1, select AIR FRY, set temperature to 200°C, and set time to 12 minutes. Select MATCH COOK to match Zone 2 settings to Zone 1. Select START/PAUSE to begin cooking.
4. When cooking is complete, transfer prawns to a plate. Drizzle with lemon juice to serve hot.

Cajun Spiced Salmon

Prep time: 10 minutes, Cook time: 12 minutes, Serves 2

2 (200 g) (2 cm thick) salmon illets
½ tsp. coconut sugar

1 tbsp. Cajun seasoning
1 tbsp. fresh lemon juice

1. Season the salmon evenly with Cajun seasoning and coconut sugar.
2. Install a crisper plate in a basket. Place salmon fillets in the basket, skin-side up, then insert basket in unit.
3. Select Zone 1, select AIR FRY, set temperature to 200℃, and set time to 12 minutes. Press the START/PAUSE button to begin cooking.
4. When cooking is complete, remove basket from unit. Transfer salmon fillets to a plate. Drizzle with the lemon juice and serve hot.

Delicious Prawns and Sweet Potatoes

Prep time: 20 minutes, Cook time: 25 minutes, Serves 4

1 shallot, chopped   4 lemon grass stalks
1 red chilli pepper, seeded and chopped finely
12 king prawns, peeled and deveined
5 large sweet potatoes, peeled and cut into slices

2 tbsps. dried rosemary   ¹80 ml olive oil, divided
4 garlic cloves, minced   1 tbsp. honey
Smoked paprika, to taste

1. Mix 60ml of the olive oil, shallot, red chilli pepper, garlic and paprika in a bowl.
2. Add prawns and coat evenly with the mixture.
3. Thread the prawns onto lemongrass stalks and refrigerate to marinate for about 3 hours.
4. Mix sweet potatoes, honey and rosemary in a bowl and toss to coat well.
5. Install a crisper plate in both baskets. Place prawns in the Zone 1 basket, then insert basket in unit. Place sweet potatoes in the Zone 2 basket, then insert basket in unit.
6. Select Zone 1, select AIR FRY, set temperature to 200℃, and set time to 13 minutes. Select Zone 2, select AIR FRY, set temperature to 200℃, and set time to 25 minutes. Select SMART FINISH. Press the START/PAUSE button to begin cooking.
7. When the Zone 1 and 2 times reach 7 minutes, press START/PAUSE to pause the unit. Remove the baskets from unit and shake for 10 seconds. Reinsert baskets in unit and press START/PAUSE to resume cooking.
8. When cooking is complete, serve prawns immediately with sweet potatoes.

CHAPTER 5 PORK

Caramelized Pork

Prep time: 10 minutes, Cook time: 15 minutes, Serves 6

1 kg pork shoulder, cut into 4 cm thick slices
80 ml soy sauce   2 tbsps. sugar   1 tbsp. honey

1. Mix all the ingredients in a large bowl and coat chops well.
2. Cover and refrigerate for about 8 hours.
3. Install a crisper plate in both baskets. Place half of pork in each basket.
4. Select Zone 1, select ROAST, set temperature to 200℃, and set time to 15 minutes. Select MATCH COOK to match Zone 2 settings to Zone 1. Select START/PAUSE to begin cooking.
5. When the Zone 1 and 2 times reach 8 minutes, press START/PAUSE to pause the unit. Remove the baskets from unit and flip the pork over. Reinsert baskets in unit and press START/PAUSE to resume cooking.
6. When cooking is complete, transfer pork to a plate. Serve warm.

Pork Tenderloin with Bacon and Veggies

Prep time: 20 minutes, Cook time: 40 minutes, Serves 3

3 potatoes   350 g frozen green beans   2 tbsps. olive oil
6 bacon slices   3 (180 g) pork tenderloins

1. Pierce the potatoes with a fork.
2. Wrap 4-6 green beans with one bacon slice and coat the pork tenderloins with olive oil.
3. Install a crisper plate in both baskets. Place potatoes in the Zone 1 basket, then insert basket in unit. Place pork tenderloins in the Zone 2 basket, then insert basket in unit.
4. Select Zone 1, select ROAST, set temperature to 200℃, and set time to 40 minutes. Select Zone 2, select AIR FRY, set temperature to 190°C and set time to 25 minutes. Press the START/PAUSE button to begin cooking.
5. When the Zone 2 time reaches zero, gently transfer pork tenderloins to a serving dish and cut into desired size slices.
6. Arrange the bean rolls in the Zone 2 basket, then insert basket in unit. Select Zone 2, select AIR FRY, set temperature to 200℃, and set time to 15 minutes.
7. When cooking is complete, transfer potatoes and bean rolls to a plate. Then preheat the pork tenderloins. Serve warm.

Herbed Pork Burgers

Prep time: 15 minutes, Cook time: 15 minutes, Serves 8

2 small onions, chopped

2 tsps. fresh basil, chopped

40 g cheddar cheese, grated

2 tsps. mustard   2 tsps. garlic puree

2 tsps. tomato puree

Salt and freshly ground black pepper, to taste

2 tsps. dried mixed herbs, crushed

600 g pork mince

8 burger buns

1. Mix all the ingredients in a bowl except cheese and buns.
2. Make 8 equal-sized patties from the pork mixture.
3. Install a crisper plate in both baskets. Place 4 patties in a single layer in each basket.
4. Select Zone 1, select AIR FRY, set temperature to 200°C and set time to 15 minutes. Select MATCH COOK to match Zone 2 settings to Zone 1. Select START/PAUSE to begin cooking.
5. When the Zone 1 and 2 times reach 6 minutes, press START/PAUSE to pause the unit. Remove the baskets from unit and flip the patties over. Reinsert baskets in unit and press START/PAUSE to resume cooking.
6. When cooking is complete, arrange the patties in buns with cheese to serve.

Flavoursome Pork Chops with Peanut Sauce

Prep time: 30 minutes, Cook time: 15 minutes, Serves 4

For the Pork:

500 g pork chops, cubed into 2.5 cm size

1 tsp. fresh ginger, minced

1 garlic clove, minced

2 tbsps. soy sauce   1 tbsp. olive oil

1 tsp. hot pepper sauce

For Peanut Sauce:

2 tbsps. olive oil, divided   1 shallot, chopped finely

1 garlic clove, minced   1 tsp. ground coriander

1 tsp. hot pepper sauce   100 g ground peanuts

180 ml coconut milk

1. For the Pork: Mix all the ingredients in a bowl and keep aside for about 30 minutes.
2. Install a crisper plate in a basket. Place chops in the basket, then insert basket in unit.
3. Select Zone 1, select AIR FRY, set temperature to 200°C, and set time to 15 minutes. Press the START/PAUSE button to begin cooking.
4. With 7 minutes remaining, press START/PAUSE to pause the unit. Remove the basket from unit and flip the chops over. Reinsert basket in unit and press START/PAUSE to resume cooking.
5. For the Peanut Sauce: Heat 1 tbsp. olive oil in a pan on medium heat and add shallot and garlic. Sauté for about 3 minutes and stir in coriander. Sauté for about 1 minute and add rest of the ingredients. Cook for about 5 minutes.
6. When cooking is complete, remove basket from unit. Transfer pork chops to a plate. Pour the peanut sauce over the pork chops to serve.

Pepperoni and Bell Pepper Pockets

Prep time: 5 minutes, Cook time: 10 minutes, Serves 4

4 bread slices, 2.5 cm thick
Olive oil, for misting
24 slices pepperoni

30 g roasted red peppers, drained and patted dry
30 g Pepper Jack cheese, cut into 4 slices

1. Spray both sides of bread slices with olive oil.
2. Stand slices upright and cut a deep slit in the top to create a pocket (almost to the bottom crust, but not all the way through).
3. Stuff each bread pocket with 6 slices of pepperoni, a large strip of roasted red pepper, and a slice of cheese.
4. Install a crisper plate in both baskets. Place 2 bread pockets in a single layer in each basket, standing up.
5. Select Zone 1, select AIR FRY, set temperature to 180℃, and set time to 10 minutes. Select MATCH COOK to match Zone 2 settings to Zone 1. Select START/PAUSE to begin cooking.
6. When cooking is complete, transfer bread pockets to a plate. Serve warm.

Mexican Pork Chops

Prep time: 5 minutes, Cook time: 14 minutes, Serves 2

¼ tsp. dried oregano
1½ tsps. taco seasoning mix

2 (120 g) boneless pork chops
2 tbsps. unsalted butter, divided

1. Combine the dried oregano and taco seasoning in a small bowl and rub the mixture into the pork chops. Brush the chops with 1 tbsp. butter.
2. Install a crisper plate in a basket. Place pork chops in the basket, then insert basket in unit.
3. Select Zone 1, select ROAST, set temperature to 200℃, and set time to 14 minutes. Press the START/PAUSE button to begin cooking.
4. With 6 minutes remaining, press START/PAUSE to pause the unit. Remove the basket from unit and flip the pork chops over. Reinsert basket in unit and press START/PAUSE to resume cooking.
5. When cooking is complete, remove basket from unit. Transfer pork chops to a plate. Serve with a garnish of remaining butter.

Sausage Meatballs

Prep time: 15 minutes, Cook time: 14 minutes, Serves 4

100 g sausage, casing removed ½
medium onion, minced finely
1 tsp. fresh sage, chopped finely
3 tbsps. Italian breadcrumbs

½ tsp. garlic, minced
Salt and black pepper, to taste
cooking spray

1. Mix all the ingredients in a bowl until well combined.
2. Shape the mixture into equal-sized balls.
3. Install a crisper plate in a basket. Place balls in the basket, then insert basket in unit. Lightly spray with the cooking spray.
4. Select Zone 1, select AIR FRY, set temperature to 200℃, and set time to 14 minutes. Press the START/PAUSE button to begin cooking.
5. With 7 minutes remaining, press START/PAUSE to pause the unit. Remove the basket from unit and flip the balls over. Reinsert basket in unit and press START/PAUSE to resume cooking.
6. When cooking is complete, remove basket from unit. Transfer balls to a plate. Serve warm.

Tomato Stuffed Pork Roll

Prep time: 20 minutes, Cook time: 18 minutes, Serves 4

1 spring onion, chopped

20 g sun-dried tomatoes, chopped finely

2 tbsps. fresh parsley, chopped

4 (180 g) pork cutlets, pounded slightly Salt and freshly ground black pepper, to taste

2 tsps. paprika   ½ tbsp. olive oil

1. Mix spring onion, tomatoes, parsley, salt and black pepper in a bowl.
2. Coat each cutlet with tomato mixture and roll up the cutlet, securing with cocktail sticks.
3. Coat the rolls with oil and rub with paprika, salt and black pepper.
4. Install a crisper plate in both baskets. Place 2 rolls in a single layer in each basket.
5. Select Zone 1, select AIR FRY, set temperature to 200℃, and set time to 18 minutes. Select MATCH COOK to match Zone 2 settings to Zone 1. Select START/PAUSE to begin cooking.
6. When the Zone 1 and 2 times reach 8 minutes, press START/PAUSE to pause the unit. Remove the baskets from unit and flip the rolls over. Reinsert baskets in unit and press START/PAUSE to resume cooking.
7. When cooking is complete, transfer rolls to a plate. Serve warm.

Pork Tenderloin with Bell Peppers

Prep time: 20 minutes, Cook time: 22 minutes, Serves 3

1 large red bell pepper, seeded and cut into thin strips

1 red onion, thinly sliced

300 g pork tenderloin, cut into 4 pieces

2 tsps. Herbs de Provence

Salt and ground black pepper, as required

1 tbsp. olive oil   ½ tbsp. Dijon mustard

1. Mix the bell pepper, onion, Herbs de Provence, salt, black pepper, and ½ tbsp. of oil in a bowl.
2. Rub the tenderloin evenly with mustard, salt, and black pepper and drizzle with the remaining oil.
3. Install a crisper plate in both baskets. Place bell pepper mixture in the Zone 1 basket, then insert basket in unit. Place pork tenderloin in the Zone 2 basket, then insert basket in unit.
4. Select Zone 1, select ROAST, set temperature to 200℃, and set time to 15 minutes. Select Zone 2, select AIR FRY, set temperature to 190°C and set time to 22 minutes. Select SMART FINISH. Press the START/PAUSE button to begin cooking.
5. When the Zone 1 and 2 times reach 8 minutes, press START/PAUSE to pause the unit. Remove the baskets from unit and flip the tenderloin and bell pepper mixture over. Reinsert baskets in unit and press START/PAUSE to resume cooking.
6. When cooking is complete, dish out the tenderloin and cut into desired size slices. Serve with bell pepper.

Bacon-Wrapped Jalapeño Poppers

Prep time: 5 minutes, Cook time: 16 minutes, Serves 6

6 large jalapeños
110 g ⅓-less-fat cream cheese
20 g shredded reduced-fat sharp Cheddar cheese
2 spring onions, green tops only, sliced
6 slices centre-cut bacon, halved

1. Wearing rubber gloves, halve the jalapeños lengthwise to make 12 pieces. Scoop out the seeds and membranes and discard.

2. In a medium bowl, combine the cream cheese, Cheddar, and spring onions. Using a small spoon or spatula, fill the jalapeños with the cream cheese filling. Wrap a bacon strip around each pepper and secure with a toothpick.

3. Install a crisper plate in both baskets. Place half of stuffed peppers in a single layer in each basket.

4. Select Zone 1, select AIR FRY, set temperature to 200°C and set time to 16 minutes. Select MATCH COOK to match Zone 2 settings to Zone 1. Select START/PAUSE to begin cooking, until the peppers are tender, the bacon is browned and crisp, and the cheese is melted.

5. When cooking is complete, transfer stuffed peppers to a plate. Serve warm.

Pork Neck Salad

Prep time: 20 minutes, Cook time: 14 minutes, Serves 2

250 g pork neck   1 red onion, sliced   1 bunch fresh basil leaves
1 ripe tomato, thickly sliced   1 tbsp. soy sauce   1 tbsp. fish sauce
1 spring onion, chopped ½ tbsp. oyster sauce

1. Mix all the sauces in a bowl and coat the pork neck in it. Refrigerate for about 3 hours.

2. Install a crisper plate in a basket. Place pork neck in the basket, then insert basket in unit.

3. Select Zone 1, select AIR FRY, set temperature to 190°C, and set time to 14 minutes. Press the START/PAUSE button to begin cooking.

4. With 7 minutes remaining, press START/PAUSE to pause the unit. Remove the basket from unit and flip the pork neck over. Reinsert basket in unit and press START/PAUSE to resume cooking.

5. When cooking is complete, remove basket from unit. Transfer pork neck to a plate. Cut into desired size slices and keep aside.

6. Mix rest of the ingredients in a bowl and top with the pork slices to serve.

Air Fried Baby Back Ribs

Prep time: 5 minutes, Cook time: 30 minutes, Serves 2

2 tsps. red pepper flakes

¾ ground ginger

3 cloves minced garlic

2 baby back ribs

Salt and ground black pepper, to taste

1. Combine the red pepper flakes, ginger, garlic, salt and pepper in a bowl, making sure to mix well. Massage the mixture into the baby back ribs.
2. Install a crisper plate in a basket. Place baby back ribs in the basket, then insert basket in unit.
3. Select Zone 1, select AIR FRY, set temperature to 190℃, and set time to 30 minutes. Press the START/PAUSE button to begin cooking.
4. With 15 minutes remaining, press START/PAUSE to pause the unit. Remove the basket from unit and flip the baby back ribs over. Reinsert basket in unit and press START/PAUSE to resume cooking.
5. When cooking is complete, remove basket from unit. Transfer baby back ribs to a plate. Serve warm.

Cheesy Sausage Balls

Prep time: 5 minutes, Cook time: 17 minutes, Serves 6

350 g Jimmy Dean's Sausage

180 g shredded Cheddar cheese

10 Cheddar cubes

1. Mix the shredded cheese and sausage.
2. Divide the mixture into 12 equal parts to be stuffed.
3. Add a cube of cheese to the centre of the sausage and roll into balls.
4. Install a crisper plate in both baskets. Place half of balls in a single layer in each basket.
5. Select Zone 1, select AIR FRY, set temperature to 190℃, and set time to 17 minutes. Select MATCH COOK to match Zone 2 settings to Zone 1. Select START/PAUSE to begin cooking.
6. When the Zone 1 and 2 times reach 8 minutes, press START/PAUSE to pause the unit. Remove the baskets from unit and flip the balls over. Reinsert baskets in unit and press START/PAUSE to resume cooking.
7. When cooking is complete, transfer balls to a plate. Serve warm.

BBQ Pork Steaks

Prep time: 5 minutes, Cook time: 17 minutes, Serves 4

4 pork steaks

1 tbsp. Cajun seasoning

1 tsp. soy sauce

100 g brown sugar

2 tbsps. BBQ sauce

1 tbsp. vinegar

100 g ketchup

1. Sprinkle pork steaks with Cajun seasoning.
2. Combine remaining ingredients and brush onto steaks.
3. Install a crisper plate in both baskets. Place 2 steaks in a single layer in each basket.
4. Select Zone 1, select AIR FRY, set temperature to 200℃, and set time to 17 minutes. Select MATCH COOK to match Zone 2 settings to Zone 1. Select START/PAUSE to begin cooking.
5. When the Zone 1 and 2 times reach 8 minutes, press START/PAUSE to pause the unit. Remove the baskets from unit and flip the steaks over. Reinsert baskets in unit and press START/PAUSE to resume cooking.
6. When cooking is complete, transfer steaks to a plate. Serve warm.

CHAPTER 6 BEEF

Braising Steak with Brussels Sprouts

Prep time: 20 minutes, Cook time: 25 minutes, Serves 4

500 g beef braising shoulder steak

2 tbsps. vegetable oil   1 tbsp. red wine vinegar

1 tsp. fine sea salt   ½ tsp. ground black pepper

1 tsp. smoked paprika   1 tsp. onion powder

½ tsp. garlic powder   1 tsp. dried sage

250 g Brussels sprouts, cleaned and halved ½ tsp.

fennel seeds   1 tsp. dried basil

1. Massage the beef with the vegetable oil, wine vinegar, salt, black pepper, paprika, onion powder, and garlic powder, coating it well.

2. Allow to marinate for a minimum of 3 hours.

3. Install a crisper plate in both baskets. Remove the beef from the marinade and put in the Zone 1 basket, then insert basket in unit. Place Brussels sprouts in the Zone 2 basket along with the fennel seeds, basil, and sage, then insert basket in unit.

4. Select Zone 1, select ROAST, set temperature to 200°C, and set time to 20 minutes. Select Zone 2, select AIR FRY, set temperature to 200°C, and set time to 25 minutes. Select SMART FINISH. Press the START/PAUSE button to begin cooking.

5. When the Zone 1 and Zone 2 times reach 10 minutes, press START/PAUSE and remove baskets from unit. In Zone 1, flip the beef over. In Zone 2, shake for 10 seconds. Reinsert baskets in unit and press START/PAUSE to resume cooking.

6. When cooking is complete, serve beef with Brussels sprouts.

Classic Flank Steak Strips with Veggies

Prep time: 10 minutes, Cook time: 17 minutes, Serves 4

1 (350 g) flank steak, cut into thin strips   60 ml olive oil, divided   2 tbsps. soy sauce

250 g fresh mushrooms, quartered   2 tbsps. honey

180 g snow peas   1 onion, cut into half rings   Salt and black pepper, to taste

1. Mix 2 tbsps. of oil, soy sauce and honey in a bowl and coat steak strips with this marinade.

2. Put vegetables, remaining oil, salt and black pepper in another bowl and toss well.

3. Install a crisper plate in both baskets. Place steak strips in the Zone 1 basket, then insert basket in unit. Place vegetables in the Zone 2 basket, then insert basket in unit.

4. Select Zone 1, select AIR FRY, set temperature to 200°C, and set time to 17 minutes. Select Zone 2, select AIR FRY, set temperature to 200°C, and set time to 15 minutes. Select SMART FINISH. Press the START/PAUSE button to begin cooking.

5. When the Zone 1 and 2 times reach 8 minutes, press START/PAUSE to pause the unit. Remove the baskets from unit and shake for 10 seconds. Reinsert baskets in unit and press START/PAUSE to resume cooking.

6. When cooking is complete, serve steak strips with vegetables.

Rosemary Ribeye Steaks

Prep time: 10 minutes, Cook time: 16 minutes, Serves 2

60 g butter   1 clove garlic, minced
Salt and ground black pepper, to taste
1½ tbsps. balsamic vinegar
20 g rosemary, chopped   2 ribeye steaks

1. Melt the butter in a frying pan over medium heat. Add the garlic and fry until fragrant.
2. Remove the frying pan from the heat and add the salt, pepper, and vinegar. Allow it to cool.
3. Add the rosemary, then pour the mixture into a Ziploc bag.
4. Put the ribeye steaks in the bag and shake well, coating the meat well. Refrigerate for an hour, then allow to sit for a further 20 minutes.
5. Install a crisper plate in a basket. Place ribeyes in the basket, then insert basket in unit.
6. Select Zone 1, select AIR FRY, set temperature to 200°C, and set time to 16 minutes. Press the START/PAUSE button to begin cooking.
7. With 8 minutes remaining, press START/PAUSE to pause the unit. Remove the basket from unit and flip the ribeyes over. Reinsert basket in unit and press START/PAUSE to resume cooking.
8. When cooking is complete, remove basket from unit. Transfer ribeyes to a plate. Serve warm.

Simple Beef Burgers

Prep time: 20 minutes, Cook time: 16 minutes, Serves 6

1 kg beef mince   6 tbsps. tomato ketchup
120 g cheddar cheese slices   12 dinner rolls   Salt and black pepper, to taste

1. Mix the beef, salt and black pepper in a bowl.
2. Make small equal-sized patties from the beef mixture.
3. Install a crisper plate in both baskets. Place half of patties in a single layer in each basket.
4. Select Zone 1, select BAKE, set temperature to 200°C, and set time to 16 minutes. Select MATCH COOK to match Zone 2 settings to Zone 1. Select START/PAUSE to begin cooking.
5. When the Zone 1 and 2 times reach 8 minutes, press START/PAUSE to pause the unit. Remove the baskets from unit and flip the patties over. Reinsert baskets in unit and press START/PAUSE to resume cooking.
6. When cooking is complete, transfer pork chops to a plate. top each patty with 1 cheese slice. Arrange the patties between rolls and drizzle with ketchup. Serve hot.

Mushroom and Beef Meatloaf

Prep time: 10 minutes, Cook time: 25 minutes, Serves 4

500 g beef mince

1 egg, beaten   100 g mushrooms, sliced

1 tbsp. thyme   1 small onion, chopped

3 tbsps. bread crumbs

Ground black pepper, to taste

1. Put all the ingredients into a large bowl and combine entirely.
2. Transfer the meatloaf mixture into the loaf pan.
3. Install a crisper plate in a basket. Place loaf pan in the basket, then insert basket in unit.
4. Select Zone 1, select BAKE, set temperature to 200℃, and set time to 25 minutes. Press the START/PAUSE button to begin cooking.
5. When cooking is complete, remove the meatloaf from unit. Slice up before serving.

Bacon-Wrapped Beef Hot Dog

Prep time: 5 minutes, Cook time: 12 minutes, Serves 4

4 slices sugar-free bacon

4 beef hot dogs

1. Take a slice of bacon and wrap it around the hot dog, securing it with a toothpick. Repeat with the other pieces of bacon and hot dogs.
2. Install a crisper plate in a basket. Place wrapped dogs in the basket, then insert basket in unit.
3. Select Zone 1, select AIR FRY, set temperature to 200℃, and set time to 12 minutes. Press the START/PAUSE button to begin cooking.
4. With 6 minutes remaining, press START/PAUSE to pause the unit. Remove the basket from unit and flip the wrapped dogs over. Reinsert basket in unit and press START/PAUSE to resume cooking.
5. When cooking is complete, remove basket from unit. Transfer wrapped dogs to a plate. Serve warm.

Avocado Buttered Flank Steak

Prep time: 5 minutes, Cook time: 12 minutes, Serves 1

1 flank steak   120 ml chimichurri sauce   2 avocados   2 tbsps. butter, melted
Salt and ground black pepper, to taste

1. Rub the flank steak with salt and pepper to taste and leave to sit for 20 minutes.
2. Halve the avocados and take out the pits. Spoon the flesh into a bowl and mash with a fork. Mix in the melted butter and chimichurri sauce, making sure everything is well combined.
3. Install a crisper plate in a basket. Place steak in the basket, then insert basket in unit.
4. Select Zone 1, select AIR FRY, set temperature to 200℃, and set time to 12 minutes. Press the START/PAUSE button to begin cooking.
5. With 6 minutes remaining, press START/PAUSE to pause the unit. Remove the basket from unit and flip the steak over. Reinsert basket in unit and press START/PAUSE to resume cooking.
6. When cooking is complete, remove basket from unit. Transfer steak to a plate. Serve with the avocado butter.

Steak with Bell Peppers

Prep time: 20 minutes, Cook time: 18 minutes, Serves 4

550 beef steak, cut into thin strips

2 green bell peppers, seeded and cubed

1 red bell pepper, seeded and cubed

1 red onion, sliced

1 tsp. dried oregano, crushed

1 tsp. onion powder   1 tsp. garlic powder

1 tsp. red chilli powder   1 tsp. paprika

Salt, to taste   2 tbsps. olive oil

1. Mix the oregano and spices in a bowl.

2. Add bell peppers, onion, oil, and beef strips and mix until well combined.

3. Install a crisper plate in both baskets. Place beef strips in the Zone 1 basket, then insert basket in unit. Place vegetables in the Zone 2 basket, then insert basket in unit.

4. Select Zone 1, select AIR FRY, set temperature to 200℃, and set time to 18 minutes. Select Zone 2, select AIR FRY, set temperature to 200℃, and set time to 15 minutes. Select SMART FINISH. Press the START/PAUSE button to begin cooking.

5. When the Zone 1 and 2 times reach 8 minutes, press START/PAUSE to pause the unit. Remove the baskets from unit and flip the beef strips and vegetables over. Reinsert baskets in unit and press START/PAUSE to resume cooking.

6. When cooking is complete, serve beef strips with vegetables.

Beef Short Ribs

Prep time: 15 minutes, Cook time: 18 minutes, Serves 8

2 kg bone-in beef short ribs

35 g spring onions, chopped

1 tbsp. fresh ginger, finely grated

250 ml low-sodium soy sauce

120 ml rice vinegar

1 tbsp. Sriracha

2 tbsps. brown sugar

1 tsp. ground black pepper

1. Put the ribs with all other ingredients in a resealable bag and seal the bag.

2. Shake to coat well and refrigerate overnight.

3. Install a crisper plate in both baskets. Remove the short ribs from resealable bag and arrange half of the ribs in a single layer in each basket.

4. Select Zone 1, select AIR FRY, set temperature to 200℃, and set time to 18 minutes. Select MATCH COOK to match Zone 2 settings to Zone 1. Select START/PAUSE to begin cooking.

5. When the Zone 1 and 2 times reach 8 minutes, press START/PAUSE to pause the unit. Remove the baskets from unit and flip the ribs over. Reinsert baskets in unit and press START/PAUSE to resume cooking.

6. When cooking is complete, transfer ribs to a plate. Serve warm.

Super Simple Steaks

Prep time: 5 minutes, Cook time: 14 minutes, Serves 2

250 g quality cuts steak   Salt and black pepper, to taste

1. Season the steaks evenly with salt and black pepper.
2. Install a crisper plate in a basket. Place steaks in the basket, then insert basket in unit.
3. Select Zone 1, select AIR FRY, set temperature to 200℃, and set time to 14 minutes. Press the START/PAUSE button to begin cooking.
4. With 7 minutes remaining, press START/PAUSE to pause the unit. Remove the basket from unit and flip the steaks over. Reinsert basket in unit and press START/PAUSE to resume cooking.
5. When cooking is complete, remove basket from unit. Transfer steaks to a plate. Serve warm.

Beef Meatballs

Prep time: 5 minutes, Cook time: 16 minutes, Serves 5

500 g beef mince   50 g Mozzarella cheese
50 g grated Parmesan cheese   1 tsp. freshly ground pepper
1 tbsp. minced garlic

1. In a bowl, mix all the ingredients together.
2. Roll the meat mixture into 5 generous meatballs.
3. Install a crisper plate in a basket. Place meatballs in the basket, then insert basket in unit.
4. Select Zone 1, select AIR FRY, set temperature to 200℃, and set time to 16 minutes. Press the START/PAUSE button to begin cooking.
5. With 8 minutes remaining, press START/PAUSE to pause the unit. Remove the basket from unit and flip the meatballs over. Reinsert basket in unit and press START/PAUSE to resume cooking.
6. When cooking is complete, remove basket from unit. Transfer meatballs to a plate. Serve warm.

Beef Loin with Thyme and Parsley

Prep time: 5 minutes, Cook time: 15 minutes, Serves 4

1 tbsp. butter, melted   ¼ dried thyme   500 g beef loin
1 tsp. garlic salt   ¼ tsp. dried parsley

1. In a bowl, combine the melted butter, thyme, garlic salt, and parsley.
2. Cut the beef loin into slices and generously apply the seasoned butter using a brush.
3. Install a crisper plate in a basket. Place beef loin in the basket, then insert basket in unit.
4. Select Zone 1, select AIR FRY, set temperature to 200℃, and set time to 15 minutes. Press the START/PAUSE button to begin cooking.
5. With 7 minutes remaining, press START/PAUSE to pause the unit. Remove the basket from unit and flip the beef loin over. Reinsert basket in unit and press START/PAUSE to resume cooking.
6. When cooking is complete, remove basket from unit. Transfer beef loin to a plate. Serve warm.

Flank Steak Beef

Prep time: 10 minutes, Cook time: 15 minutes, Serves 4

500 g flank steaks, sliced

60 ml Xanthum gum   2 tsps. coconut oil

½ tsp. ginger   120 ml soy sauce

1 tbsp. garlic, minced   120 ml water

150 g sweetener, packed

1. Coat the steaks with Xanthum gum on both the sides.
2. Install a crisper plate in a basket. Place steaks in the basket, then insert basket in unit.
3. Select Zone 1, select AIR FRY, set temperature to 200℃, and set time to 15 minutes. Press the START/PAUSE button to begin cooking.
4. With 6 minutes remaining, press START/PAUSE to pause the unit. Remove the basket from unit and flip the steak slices over. Reinsert basket in unit and press START/PAUSE to resume cooking.
5. When cooking is complete, remove basket from unit. Transfer the steak slices to a plate. Meanwhile, cook rest of the ingredients for the sauce in a saucepan.
6. Bring to a boil and pour over the steak slices to serve.

Perfect Flank Steak

Prep time: 15 minutes, Cook time: 15 minutes, Serves 4

25 g fresh parsley leaves, chopped finely

3 tbsps. fresh oregano, chopped finely

3 tbsps. fresh mint leaves, chopped finely

2 (250 g) flank steaks 3 garlic cloves, minced

1 tbsp. ground cumin   2 tsps. smoked paprika

1 tsp. cayenne pepper

1 tsp. red pepper flakes, crushed

Salt and freshly ground black pepper, to taste

180 ml olive oil   3 tbsps. red wine vinegar

1. Season the steaks with a little salt and black pepper.
2. Mix all the ingredients in a large bowl except the steaks.
3. Put ¼ cup of the herb mixture and steaks in a resealable bag and shake well.
4. Refrigerate for about 24 hours and reserve the remaining herb mixture.
5. Keep the steaks at room temperature for about 30 minutes.
6. Install a crisper plate in a basket. Place steaks in the basket, then insert basket in unit.
7. Select Zone 1, select ROAST, set temperature to 200℃, and set time to 15 minutes. Press the START/PAUSE button to begin cooking.
8. With 8 minutes remaining, press START/PAUSE to pause the unit. Remove the basket from unit and flip the steaks over. Reinsert basket in unit and press START/PAUSE to resume cooking.
9. When cooking is complete, remove basket from unit. Transfer steaks to a plate and sprinkle with remaining herb mixture to serve.

CHAPTER 7 SNACK AND DESSERT

Cayenne Sesame Nut Mix

Prep time: 10 minutes, Cook time: 5 minutes, Makes 4 cups

1 tbsp. buttery spread, melted

¼ tsp. cayenne pepper

¼ tsp. kosher salt

150 g cashews

150 g mini pretzels

Cooking spray

2 tsps. honey

2 tsps. sesame seeds

¼ tsp. freshly ground black pepper

150 g almonds

150 g rice squares cereal

1. In a large bowl, combine the buttery spread, honey, cayenne pepper, sesame seeds, ko[...] salt, and black pepper, then add the cashews, almonds, pretzels, and rice squares, [...] tossing to coat.
2. Install a crisper plate in a basket and spray with cooking spray. Arrange the mixture in the basket, then insert basket in unit.
3. Select Zone 1, select ROAST, set temperature to 180℃, and set time to 5 minutes. Press the START/PAUSE button to begin cooking.
4. When cooking is complete, remove basket from unit. Allow to cool for 5 minutes before serving.

Crispy Spiced Chickpeas

Prep time: 5 minutes, Cook time: 10 minutes, Makes 1½ cups

1 can (500-g) chickpeas, rinsed and dried with paper towels

1 tbsp. olive oil

½ tsp. dried parsley

½ tsp. dried rosemary

½ tsp. dried chives

¼ tsp. mustard powder ¼ tsp. sweet paprika

¼ tsp. cayenne pepper

Kosher salt and freshly ground black pepper, to taste

1. In a large bowl, combine all the ingredients, except for the kosher salt and black pepper, and toss until the chickpeas are evenly coated in the herbs and spices.
2. Install a crisper plate in a basket. Scrape the chickpeas and seasonings into the basket, then insert basket in unit.
3. Select Zone 1, select AIR FRY, set temperature to 180℃, and set time to 10 minutes. Press the START/PAUSE button to begin cooking.
4. With 5 minutes remaining, press START/PAUSE to pause the unit. Remove the basket from unit and shake for 10 seconds. Reinsert basket in unit and press START/PAUSE to resume cooking.
5. When cooking is complete, remove basket from unit. Transfer crispy chickpeas to a bowl. Sprinkle with kosher salt and black pepper and serve warm.

Spiced Sweet Potato Fries

Prep time: 10 minutes, Cook time: 15 minutes, Serves 2

2 tbsps. olive oil   1½ tsps. smoked paprika

1½ tsps. kosher salt, plus more as needed

1 tsp. chilli powder   ½ tsp. ground cumin

½ tsp. ground turmeric   ½ tsp. mustard powder

¼ tsp. cayenne pepper

2 medium sweet potatoes (about 280 g each), cut into wedges, 1 cm thick and 7 cm long

Freshly ground black pepper, to taste

160 g sour cream   1 garlic clove, grated

1. In a large bowl, combine the olive oil, paprika, salt, chilli powder, cumin, turmeric, mustard powder, and cayenne. Add the sweet potatoes, season with black pepper, and toss to evenly coat.

2. Install a crisper plate in a basket. Place sweet potatoes in the basket (save the bowl with the leftover oil and spices), then insert basket in unit.

3. Select Zone 1, select AIR FRY, set temperature to 200°C, and set time to 15 minutes. Press the START/PAUSE button to begin cooking.

4. With 7 minutes remaining, press START/PAUSE to pause the unit. Remove the basket from unit and shake for 10 seconds. Reinsert basket in unit and press START/PAUSE to resume cooking.

5. Return the potato wedges to the reserved bowl and toss again while they are hot.

6. Meanwhile, in a small bowl, stir together the sour cream and garlic. Season with salt and black pepper and transfer to a serving dish.

7. Serve the potato wedges hot with the garlic sour cream.

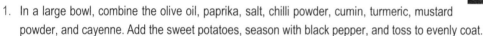

Courgette and Potato Tots

Prep time: 5 minutes, Cook time: 14 minutes, Serves 4

1 large courgette, grated   1 large egg, beaten

1 medium baked potato, skin removed and mashed   ½ tsp. kosher salt   Cooking spray

20 g shredded Cheddar cheese

1. Wrap the grated courgette in a paper towel and squeeze out any excess liquid, then combine the courgette, baked potato, shredded Cheddar cheese, egg, and kosher salt in a large bowl.

2. Spray two 18 x 12 cm baking pans with cooking spray, then place the courgette mixture in the pans.

3. Install a crisper plate in both baskets. Place one baking pan in each basket.

4. Select Zone 1, select AIR FRY, set temperature to 200°C, and set time to 14 minutes. Select MATCH COOK to match Zone 2 settings to Zone 1. Select START/PAUSE to begin cooking.

5. When cooking is complete, transfer tots to a plate and allow to cool on a wire rack for 5 minutes before serving.

Crispy Apple Chips

Prep time: 5 minutes, Cook time: 30 minutes, Serves 1

1 Honeycrisp or Pink Lady apple

1. Core the apple with an apple corer, leaving apple whole. Cut the apple into 3 mm-thick slices.
2. Install a crisper plate in a basket. Place apple slices in the basket, staggering slices as much as possible, then insert basket in unit.
3. Select Zone 1, select AIR FRY, set temperature to 150℃, and set time to 30 minutes. Press the START/PAUSE button to begin cooking, until the chips are dry and some are lightly browned, turning 4 times with tongs to separate and rotate them from top to bottom.
4. When cooking is complete, remove basket from unit. Place the chips in a single layer on a wire rack to cool. Apples will become crisper as they cool. Serve immediately.

Beef and Mango Skewers

Prep time: 10 minutes, Cook time: 10 minutes, Serves 4

350 g beef sirloin tip, cut into 2.5 cm cubes   Pinch of salt   1 mango
2 tbsps. balsamic vinegar   1 tbsp. olive oil   Freshly ground black pepper, to taste
1 tbsp. honey   ½ tsp. dried marjoram

1. Put the beef cubes in a medium bowl and add the balsamic vinegar, olive oil, honey, marjoram, salt, and pepper. Mix well, then massage the marinade into the beef with your hands. Set aside.
2. To prepare the mango, stand it on end and cut the skin off, using a sharp knife. Then carefully cut around the oval pit to remove the flesh. Cut the mango into 2.5 cm cubes.
3. Thread metal skewers alternating with three beef cubes and two mango cubes.
4. Install a crisper plate in a basket. Place skewers in the basket, then insert basket in unit.
5. Select Zone 1, select ROAST, set temperature to 200℃, and set time to 10 minutes. Press the START/PAUSE button to begin cooking.
6. With 5 minutes remaining, press START/PAUSE to pause the unit. Remove the basket from unit and flip the skewers over. Reinsert basket in unit and press START/PAUSE to resume cooking.
7. When cooking is complete, remove basket from unit. Transfer skewers to a plate. Serve warm.

Fast and Easy Tortilla Chips

Prep time: 5 minutes, Cook time: 5 minutes, Serves 2

8 corn tortillas   1 tbsp. olive oil   Salt, to taste

1. Slice the corn tortillas into triangles. Coat with a light brushing of olive oil.
2. Install a crisper plate in both baskets. Place half of the tortilla pieces in a single layer in each basket.
3. Select Zone 1, select AIR FRY, set temperature to 200°C and set time to 5 minutes. Select MATCH COOK to match Zone 2 settings to Zone 1. Select START/PAUSE to begin cooking.
4. When cooking is complete, transfer tortilla pieces to a plate. Season with salt before serving.

Air Fried Olives

Prep time: 5 minutes, Cook time: 8 minutes, Serves 4

1 (150-g) jar pitted green olives   Salt and pepper, to taste
60 g all-purpose flour Cooking spray   60 g bread crumbs   1 egg

1. Remove the olives from the jar and dry thoroughly with paper towels.
2. In a small bowl, combine the flour with salt and pepper to taste. Place the bread crumbs in another small bowl. In a third small bowl, beat the egg.
3. Dip the olives in the flour, then the egg, and then the bread crumbs.
4. Install a crisper plate in a basket and spritz with cooking spray. Place breaded olives in the basket, then insert basket in unit.
5. Select Zone 1, select AIR FRY, set temperature to 200°C, and set time to 8 minutes. Press the START/PAUSE button to begin cooking.
6. With 4 minutes remaining, press START/PAUSE to pause the unit. Remove the basket from unit and flip the breaded olives over. Reinsert basket in unit and press START/PAUSE to resume cooking.
7. When cooking is complete, remove basket from unit. Transfer breaded olives to a plate. Cool before serving.

Strawberry Cupcakes

Prep time: 10 minutes, Cook time: 10 minutes, Serves 8

For the Cupcakes: 7 tbsps. butter
2 eggs   110 g self-raising flour
60 g caster sugar   ½ tsp. vanilla essence

For the Icing:

3½ tbsps. butter   100 g icing sugar
30 g fresh strawberries, blended
1 tbsp. whipped cream   ½ tsp. pink food colour

For the Cupcakes:

1. Grease 8 muffin tins lightly.

2. Mix all the ingredients for the cupcakes in a large bowl until well combined. Transfer the mixture into muffin tins.

3. Install a crisper plate in both baskets. Place 4 muffin tins in each basket.

4. Select Zone 1, select BAKE, set temperature to 170℃, and set time to 10 minutes. Select MATCH COOK to match Zone 2 settings to Zone 1. Select START/PAUSE to begin cooking.

5. When cooking is complete, transfer muffin tins to a plate.

For the Icing:

6. Mix all the ingredients for icing in a large bowl until well combined.

7. Fill the pastry bag with icing and top each cupcake evenly with frosting to serve.

Apple Pie Crumble

Prep time: 10 minutes, Cook time: 25 minutes, Serves 4

1 (400 ml) can apple pie   9 tbsps. self-raising flour
60 g butter, softened   Pinch of salt   7 tbsps. caster sugar

1. Grease a 18 x 12 cm baking dish.

2. Mix all the ingredients in a bowl until a crumbly mixture is formed.

3. Arrange the apple pie in the baking dish and top with the mixture.

4. Install a crisper plate in a basket. Place the baking dish in the basket, then insert basket in unit.

5. Select Zone 1, select BAKE, set temperature to 160℃, and set time to 25 minutes. Press the START/PAUSE button to begin cooking.

6. When cooking is complete, remove basket from unit. Transfer the apple pie to a plate. Serve warm.

Semolina Cake

Prep time: 15 minutes, Cook time: 15 minutes, Serves 8

350 g semolina	250 ml milk	75 g walnuts, chopped	150 g sugar
250 g Greek yoghurt	2 tsps. baking powder	120 ml olive oil	Pinch of salt

1. Grease two 18 x 12 cm baking pans lightly.
2. Mix semolina, oil, milk, yoghurt and sugar in a bowl until well combined.
3. Cover the bowl and keep aside for about 15 minutes.
4. Stir in the baking soda, baking powder and salt and fold in the walnuts. Transfer the mixture into the baking pans.
5. Install a crisper plate in both baskets. Place baking pan in each basket.
6. Select Zone 1, select BAKE, set temperature to 180℃, and set time to 15 minutes. Select MATCH COOK to match Zone 2 settings to Zone 1. Select START/PAUSE to begin cooking.
7. When cooking is complete, transfer the cake to a plate. Serve warm.

Banana Split

Prep time: 10 minutes, Cook time: 12 minutes, Serves 8

Cooking spray ¼ tsp. ground cinnamon		80 g corn flour	3 tbsps. coconut oil
120 g panko bread crumbs 2 eggs		2 tbsps. walnuts, chopped	3 tbsps. sugar
4 bananas, peeled and halved lengthwise			

1. Heat coconut oil in a frying pan on medium heat and add bread crumbs.
2. Cook for 4 minutes until golden brown and transfer into a bowl.
3. Place the flour in a shallow dish and whisk the eggs in another shallow dish.
4. Coat banana slices evenly with flour and dip in eggs and dredge again in the bread crumbs.
5. Mix the sugar and cinnamon in a small bowl and sprinkle over the banana slices.
6. Install a crisper plate in both baskets. Place half of the banana slices in a single layer in each basket. Spray with cooking spray.
7. Select Zone 1, select BAKE, set temperature to 140℃, and set time to 12 minutes. Select MATCH COOK to match Zone 2 settings to Zone 1. Select START/PAUSE to begin cooking.
8. When the Zone 1 and 2 times reach 6 minutes, press START/PAUSE to pause the unit. Remove the baskets from unit and flip the banana slices over. Reinsert baskets in unit and press START/PAUSE to resume cooking.
9. When cooking is complete, transfer banana slices to a plate. Top with walnuts and serve.

Chocolate Coconut Brownies

Prep time: 15 minutes, Cook time: 15 minutes, Serves 8

120 ml coconut oil

60 g dark chocolate

200 g sugar   2½ tbsps. water

4 whisked eggs   ¼ tsp. coconut extract

¼ tsp. ground cinnamon

½ tsp. ground star anise

½ tsp. vanilla extract 1

tbsp. honey   60 g flour

60 g desiccated coconut

Sugar, for dusting

1. Melt the coconut oil and dark chocolate in the microwave.
2. Combine with the sugar, water, eggs, cinnamon, anise, coconut extract, vanilla, and honey in a large bowl.
3. Stir in the flour and desiccated coconut. Incorporate everything well.
4. Lightly grease a 18 x 12 cm baking dish with butter. Transfer the mixture to the dish.
5. Install a crisper plate in a basket. Place the baking dish in the basket, then insert basket in unit.
6. Select Zone 1, select BAKE, set temperature to 180℃, and set time to 15 minutes. Press the START/PAUSE button to begin cooking.
7. When cooking is complete, remove basket from unit and allow to cool slightly.
8. Take care when taking it out of the baking dish. Slice it into squares.

Pear and Apple Crisp

Prep time: 10 minutes, Cook time: 20 minutes, Serves 6

250 g apples, cored and chopped

250 g pears, cored and chopped

120 g flour   200 g sugar

1 tbsp. butter   1 tsp. ground cinnamon

¼ tsp. ground cloves   1 tsp. vanilla extract

40 g chopped walnuts

Whipped cream, for serving

1. Lightly grease a 18 x 12 cm baking dish and place the apples and pears inside.
2. Combine the rest of the ingredients, minus the walnuts and the whipped cream, until a coarse, crumbly texture is achieved.
3. Pour the mixture over the fruits and spread it evenly. Top with the chopped walnuts.
4. Install a crisper plate in a basket. Place the baking dish in the basket, then insert basket in unit.
5. Select Zone 1, select BAKE, set temperature to 170℃, and set time to 20 minutes. Press the START/PAUSE button to begin cooking, until the top turns golden brown.
6. Serve at room temperature with whipped cream.

Simple Pineapple Sticks

Prep time: 5 minutes, Cook time: 10 minutes, Serves 4

½ fresh pineapple, cut into sticks   25 g desiccated coconut

1. Coat the pineapple sticks in the desiccated coconut.
2. Install a crisper plate in a basket. Place pineapple sticks in the basket, then insert basket in unit.
3. Select Zone 1, select AIR FRY, set temperature to 200℃, and set time to 10 minutes. Press the START/PAUSE button to begin cooking.
4. With 5 minutes remaining, press START/PAUSE to pause the unit. Remove the basket from unit and flip the pineapple sticks over. Reinsert basket in unit and press START/PAUSE to resume cooking.
5. When cooking is complete, remove basket from unit. Transfer pineapple sticks to a plate. Serve warm.

Coconut-Coated White Chocolate Cookies

Prep time: 15 minutes, Cook time: 14 minutes, Serves 8

100 g butter   1 small egg

150 g self-raising flour   60 g caster sugar

35 g white chocolate, chopped

3 tbsps. desiccated coconut   1 tsp. vanilla extract

1. Grease two 18 x 12 cm baking dishes lightly.
2. Mix sugar and butter in a large bowl and beat till fluffy.
3. Whisk in the egg, vanilla extract, flour and chocolate and mix until well combined.
4. Place coconut in a shallow dish and make small balls from the mixture.
5. Roll the balls into coconut evenly and arrange them on baking dishes.
6. Press each ball into a cookie-like shape.
7. Install a crisper plate in both baskets. Place baking dish in each basket.
8. Select Zone 1, select BAKE, set temperature to 180℃, and set time to 14 minutes. Select MATCH COOK to match Zone 2 settings to Zone 1. Select START/PAUSE to begin cooking.
9. When the Zone 1 and 2 times reach 4 minutes, press START/PAUSE to pause the unit. Set the Air fryer to 160°C and press START/PAUSE to resume cooking.
10. When cooking is complete, transfer cookies to a plate. Serve warm.

APPENDIX 1: NINJA DUAL ZONE AIR FRYER TIMETABLE

INGREDIENT	AMOUNT	PREPARATION	TOSS IN OIL	TEMP	COOK TIME
VEGETABLES					
Asparagus	200g	Whole, stems trimmed	2 tsp	200°C	8-12 mins
Beetroot	6 small or 4 large (about 1kg)	Whole	None	200°C	35-45 mins
Bell peppers (for roasting)	2 peppers	Whole	None	200°C	16 mins
Broccoli	1 head (400g)	Cut in 2.5cm florets	1 Tbsp	200°C	9 mins
Brussel sprouts	500g	Cut in half, stem removed	1 Tbsp	200°C	15-20 mins
Butternut squash	500g-750g	Cut in 2.5cm pieces	1 Tbsp	200°C	20-25 mins
Carrots	500g	Peeled, cut in 1.5cm pieces	1 Tbsp	200°C	13-16 mins
Cauliflower	1 head (900g)	Cut in 2.5cm florets	2 Tbsp	200°C	15-20 mins
Corn on the cob	4 ears	Whole ears, husks removed	1 Tbsp	200°C	12-15 mins
Courgette	500g	Cut in quarters lengthwise, then cut in 2.5cm pieces	1 Tbsp	200°C	15-18 mins
Fine green beans	200g	Trimmed	1 Tbsp	200°C	8 mins
Kale (for crisps)	100g	Torn in pieces, stems removed	None	150°C	8 mins
Mushrooms	225g	Wiped, cut in quarters	1 Tbsp	200°C	7 mins
Potatoes, white e.g. King Edward, Maris Piper or Russet	750g	Cut in 2.5cm wedges	1 Tbsp	200°C	18-20 mins
	450g	Hand-cut chips, thin	½-3 Tbsp, vegetable oil	200°C	20-24 mins
	450g	Hand-cut chips, thick	½-3 Tbsp, vegetable oil	200°C	23-26 mins
	4 whole (200g each)	Pierced with fork 3 times	None	200°C	25 mins
Potatoes, sweet	750g	Cut in 2.5cm chunks	1 Tbsp	200°C	15-20 mins
	4 whole (225g each)	Pierced with fork 3 times	None	200°C	30-35 mins
POULTRY					
Chicken breasts	2 breasts (200g each)	None	Brushed with oil	190°C	22-25 mins
	4 breasts (150-175g each)	None	Brushed with oil	190°C	34 mins
Chicken thighs	4 thighs (200g each)	Bone in	Brushed with oil	200°C	22-28 mins
	4 thighs (100g each)	Boneless	Brushed with oil	200°C	18-22 mins
Chicken wings	1kg	Drumettes & flats	1 Tbsp	200°C	33 mins
FISH & SEAFOOD					
Fish cakes	2 cakes (145g each)	None	Brushed with oil	200°C	15 mins
Salmon fillets	2 fillets	None	Brushed with oil	200°C	10-13 mins
Prawns	16 large	Whole, peeled, tails on	1 Tbsp	200°C	7-10 mins

INGREDIENT	AMOUNT	PREPARATION	TOSS IN OIL	TEMP	COOK TIME
BEEF					
Burgers	4 quarter-pounders	2.5cm thick	None	190°C	12 mins
Steaks	2 steaks (230g each)	Whole	None	200°C	22 mins
PORK					
Bacon	4 strips, cut in half	None	None	180°C	9 mins
Pork chops	2 thick-cut, bone-in chops	Bone in	Brushed with oil	190°C	19 mins
	4 boneless chops	Boneless	Brushed with oil	190°C	18 mins
Pork loin steaks	2 steaks (400g)	Whole	Brushed with oil	180°C	17 mins
Sausages	4 sausages	Whole	None	200°C	16 mins
Gammon steaks	1 steak (225g)	Cut rind at 2cm, turn over after 5 mins	Brushed with oil	180°C	10 mins
LAMB					
Lamb chops	4 chops (340g)	None	Brushed with oil	200°C	12 mins
Lamb steaks	3 steaks (300g)	None	Brushed with oil	200°C	12 mins
FROZEN FOODS					
Chicken nuggets	1 box (397g)	None	None	200°C	16 mins
Breaded fish fillets	4 fillets (Total 500g)	None	None	200°C	14-16 mins
Fish fingers	10	None	None	200°C	15 mins
French fries	500g	None	None	180°C	20 mins
French fries	1kg	None	None	180°C	42 mins
Sweet potato chips	450g	None	None	190°C	20 mins
Hash browns	7	Single layer	None	200°C	15 mins
Fish fillets in batter	4	Turn halfway	None	180°C	18 mins
Scampi in breadcrumbs	280g	None	None	180°C	12 mins
Prawn tempura	8 prawns (total 140g)	Turn halfway	None	190°C	8-9 mins
Chunky oven chips	500g	None	None	180°C	20 mins
Potato wedges	500g	None	None	180°C	20 mins
Roast potatoes	700g	None	None	190°C	20 mins
Vegan burgers	4	Single layer	None	180°C	10 mins
Battered onion rings	300g	None	None	190°C	14 mins
Breaded garlic mushrooms	300g	None	None	190°C	10-12 mins
Chicken goujons	11	None	None	190°C	8 mins
Chicken Kiev	4	None	None	180°C	15 mins
Yorkshire pudding	8 (total 150g)	None	None	180°C	3-4 mins

Max Crisp Cooking Chart

INGREDIENT	AMOUNT	PREPARATION	TEMP	DEHYDRATE TIME
FROZEN FOOD				
Chicken nuggets	350g (24 nuggets)	None	None	10 mins
Chicken wings	1kg	None	1 Tbsp	17 mins
Popcorn chicken	850g	None	None	6-8 mins
Sweet potato fries	500g	None	1 Tbsp	17 mins
French fries	500g	None	None	8 mins
French fries	1kg	None	None	25 mins
Onion rings	300g	None	None	9 mins

Dehydrate Chart

INGREDIENTS	PREPARATION	TEMP	DEHYDRATE TIME
FRUITS & VEGETABLES			
Apples	Core removed, cut in 3mm slices, rinsed in lemon water, patted dry	60°C	7-8 hours
Asparagus	Cut in 2.5cm pieces, blanched	60°C	6-8 hours
Bananas	Peeled, cut in 3mm slices	60°C	8-10 hours
Beetroot	Peeled, cut in 3mm slices	60°C	6-8 hours
Aubergine	Peeled, cut in 3mm slices, blanched	60°C	6-8 hours
Fresh herbs	Rinsed, patted dry, stems removed	60°C	4 hours
Ginger root	Cut in 3mm slices	60°C	6 hours
Mangoes	Peeled, cut in 3mm slices, pit removed	60°C	6-8 hours
Mushrooms	Cleaned with soft brush (do not wash)	60°C	6-8 hours
Pineapple	Peeled, cored, cut in 3mm-1.25cm slices	60°C	6-8 hours
Strawberries	Cut in half or in 1.25cm slices	60°C	6-8 hours
Tomatoes	Cut in 3mm slices or grated; steam if planning to rehydrate	60°C	6-8 hours
MEAT, POULTRY, FISH			
Beef jerky	Cut in 6mm slices, marinated overnight	70°C	5-7 hours
Chicken jerky	Cut in 6mm slices, marinated overnight	70°C	5-7 hours
Salmon jerky	Cut in 6mm slices, marinated overnight	70°C	3-5 hours
Turkey jerky	Cut in 6mm slices, marinated overnight	70°C	5-7 hours

NOTE There is no temperature adjustment available or necessary when using the Max Crisp function.

APPENDIX 2: RECIPES INDEX

Printed in Great Britain
by Amazon

24931784R00044